Succeed in
IELTS Speaking & Vocabulary

ideal for both the Academic & the General Training modules

TELEPHONE

Andrew Betsis
Sula Delafuente
Sean Haughton

GlobalELT
ENGLISH LANGUAGE TEACHING BOOKS

Introduction

IELTS is the International English Language Testing System. It tests all four language skills: listening, reading, writing and speaking. It is intended for people who want to study or work in an English-speaking country.

There are **two** versions of the test, the **Academic** and the **General Training** module. The Academic module is for those who want to study or train in an English-speaking university. University admission to undergraduate and postgraduate courses is based on the results of the Academic test.

The **General Training** module is mainly for those who are going to English-speaking countries to do secondary education or get a job and focuses on basic survival skills in social and workplace environments.

The **Speaking test** is the **same** for both the **Academic** and the **General Training** **modules**, so this book is appropriate for candidates preparing for either of the two versions of the IELTS exam.

The Speaking test consists of a discussion with an examiner and lasts 11 - 14 minutes with three parts. In Part 1, candidates have to answer personal questions about themselves and their families. In Part 2, they have to speak about a topic and in Part 3, they have a longer discussion on the same topic.

Contents

Published by GLOBAL ELT LTD
www.globalelt.co.uk
Copyright © **GLOBAL ELT LTD, 2012**

Every effort has been made to trace the copyright holders and we apologise in advance for any unintentional omission.
We will be happy to insert the appropriate acknowledgements in any subsequent editions.

British Library Cataloguing-in-Publication Data
A catalogue record of this book is available from the British Library.

● Succeed in IELTS Speaking - Student's Book - ISBN: 978-1-78164-015-9
● Succeed in IELTS Speaking - Teacher's Book - ISBN: 978-1-78164-016-6
● Succeed in IELTS Speaking - Self-Study Edition - ISBN: 978-1-78164-017-3

The authors and publishers wish to acknowledge the following use of material:
The photos in Units 1- 10 © Ingram Publishing Image Library - © www.123rf.com Image Library

IELTS FORMAT

Academic Module	General Training Module
For entry to undergraduate or postgraduate studies or for professional reasons.	For entry to vocational or training programmes not at degree level, for admission to secondary school and for immigration purposes.

The test Modules are taken in the following order:

MODULE	QUESTIONS	TIME	QUESTION TYPES
Listening	4 sections, 40 items	*approximately* 30 minutes	multiple choice, short-answer questions, sentence completion, notes, form, table, summary, flow-chart completion, labelling a diagram/map/plan, classification, matching
Academic Reading	3 sections, 40 items	60 minutes	multiple choice, short-answer questions, sentence completion, notes, form, table, summary, flow-chart completion, labelling a diagram/map/plan, classification, matching, choosing suitable paragraph headings, identification of author's views, -yes, no, not given, -true, false, not given questions
General Training Reading	3 sections, 40 items	60 minutes	
Academic Writing	2 tasks	60 minutes	**Task 1** (150 Words - 20 minutes) Candidates have to look at a diagram, chart, or graph and present the information in their own words. **Task 2** (250 Words - 40 minutes) Candidates have to present a solution to a problem or present and justify an opinion.
General Training Writing	2 tasks	60 minutes	**Task 1** (150 Words - 20 minutes) Candidates have to respond to a problem with a letter asking for information. **Task 2** (250 Words - 40 minutes) Candidates have to present a solution to a problem or present and justify an opinion.
Speaking		11 to 14 minutes	It consists of three parts; **Part 1** - Introduction and interview, **Part 2** - Long turn, **Part 3** - Discussion.
		Total Test Time 2 hours 44 minutes	

Chapter 1

IELTS Speaking Exam Guide

Speaking Test Assessment

The IELTS Speaking test is assessed using the following four criteria:

Fluency and Coherence	• Have you answered the question directly? • Can you logically support what you are talking about? • Can you carry on speaking without hesitating or correcting yourself? • Do you use different discourse markers to start your sentences?
Lexical Resource	• How wide is your vocabulary range? • Are you using the correct words for the topic and situation? • How often do you use collocation and idiomatic language?
Grammatical Range and Accuracy	• How regularly can you speak without making mistakes? • How often do you use complex sentences accurately when you speak?
Pronunciation	• Can you pronounce the sounds of English accurately? • Are your stress and intonation patterns natural? • Can you separate your language into meaningful parts? • Can most of what you say be clearly understood?

Understanding the Test

EXAM INFORMATION: The speaking test is divided into 3 sections.

Part 1 lasts about 4-5 minutes. You will be asked a number of questions about a range of personal topics.

Part 2 lasts about 3-4 minutes. You will be given a topic. You will be given 1 minute to make notes and prepare what you are going to say. You will talk about yourself and your experiences.

Part 3 lasts about 4-5 minutes. You will be asked some general questions linked to the topic you spoke about in Part 2.

EXAM STRATEGY

Try and make sure that your language changes with the test. It should become more formal and impersonal as the test progresses. **Listen** to the examiner's questions to help you know when to change your speaking style.

L1 **Listen to a candidate talking about the IELTS test**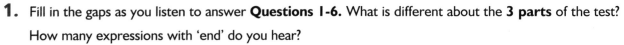

1. Fill in the gaps as you listen to answer **Questions 1-6.** What is different about the **3 parts** of the test? How many expressions with 'end' do you hear?

Although I'd practised for hours **1**........................., I was still quite nervous before my speaking test because I didn't know what to expect. **2**........................... it was really not as bad as I thought it would be. In Parts 1 and 2 the topics were much more **3**.................... and I mostly spoke about myself, my family, friends and experiences I'd had. I did notice the test changed in Part 3; the questions seemed more formal to me and I had to speak more about **4**............... and **5**................. issues. I suppose **6** .... it was like any interview; I had to listen carefully to the questions and make sure my answers were clear.

2. Match the example responses in **Column B** to the appropriate part of the IELTS Speaking test in **Column A**.

Column A	ANSWER	Column B
Part 1		1 When I think about old buildings, one particular building springs to mind. It is in the north of my country and I went there with my family last year.
		2 The way I see it, music and culture cannot be separated, but then again, it does also depend on other factors like age and how you were brought up.
Part 2		3 Teachers need to be more aware of how their behaviour can affect the way their students learn. My own personal experiences and those of my friends certainly proved that this is the case. Like many others, we had teachers whose methods actually made us not want to learn.
		4 I absolutely hate cooking! I'll make up any excuse not to have to do it.
Part 3		5 I'm going to talk about the friend I spend most time with. I've known her since I was a child. In fact, our mothers were close friends, so we probably saw each other most weekends.
		6 Well, I've been doing the same job now for about 10 years. I'm a doctor and I work in a general hospital, but I also run my own private clinic.

Chapter 2

PART 1
Introduction

The speaking test begins with introductions.

- The examiner introduces himself/herself. *'Good morning. My name is Cynthia Brown. I'll be your examiner.'*
- The examiner asks for your name. *'Can you tell me your name please?'*
  DO NOT SPELL YOUR NAME. DO NOT GIVE EXTRA INFORMATION ABOUT YOUR NAME.
- The examiner asks for identification. *'Can I see your identification please?'*
  DO NOT FORGET TO TAKE YOUR PASSPORT OR ID CARD INTO THE TEST ROOM.

1 Read the following introduction to an IELTS speaking test. Underline the five mistakes in the candidates' response.

Examiner: *Can you tell me your name please?*

Candidate: *My name is Donciano Delafuente. You spell that D-E-L-A-F-U-E-N-T-E. It means 'of the fountain' and it is an old Spanish name, which is quite interesting as my family actually comes from Italy. I'm 28 years old and I'm single.*

Give relevant answers

Your responses must directly answer the examiner's question.
Read the following questions. Which response, A, B, C or D, completely answers the question?

1. Question: What time do you like getting up in the morning?
a) I really hate getting up in the morning.
b) I have no idea.
c) I have to get up really early because I'm a doctor so I usually get up around 6.30, but if I had the choice, I'd prefer to get up at 9 o'clock.
d) I am a single mum so I have to get up at 5.00. I make breakfast for my children. Then I have to get my children ready for school. I get them dressed and take them to school and then I go to work. I drive to work and the traffic is always bad in my city so it takes me a really long time to get there.

2. Question: How often do you use the library?
a) Not as much as I should, but I try to go at least once a week.
b) I'm a teacher and I make sure my students go to the library every day because I know how important that is for them and for their learning.
c) I think libraries are so important for us.
d) We have the internet now so I don't believe people see the need to go to libraries anymore. It's really a bad thing.

3. Question: Do you think it's important to make plans?
a) Of course, why not?
b) I have made an important plan recently. I'm going to my new job in Australia so that's why this IELTS is very important for me. I need level 7. It's really necessary for me and my family.
c) I'm an English teacher, so I have to make lesson plans every day. It's an essential part of my job.
d) Absolutely. A plan is what gives you direction. I think we probably save a lot of time by making plans before we do something.

IELTS Speaking Exam Guide

EXAM TIP

DO NOT try to influence the examiner. It won't work!
[See **3 b)** on page 7] Each question needs a **DIRECT** answer.
DO NOT ignore what the examiner asks. Your job, your university major, your age, your position and your marital status is **NOT** relevant unless directly asked for.
Example: 3 c) on page 7, does not answer the given question.
It is an answer to the following question:
Question: What is your job and do you need to make plans as part of your work?

2 L2 Listen to three candidates answering Part 1 questions below. Which responses logically answer the questions (**A**) and which ones go off-topic (**O**)? Write an **A** or **O** next to each speaker.

> Was it difficult to get accepted on this course?
> Will you have to study more before you start working?

Speaker 1:   Question 1 _____   Question 2 _____

Speaker 2:   Question 1 _____   Question 2 _____

Speaker 3:   Question 1 _____   Question 2 _____

EXAM TIP

In **Part 1** the examiner cannot explain the questions; they can only repeat them.
Check you have understood by asking yes/no questions like:
Question: Will you have to study more before you start working?
* '*Do you mean* will I need work experience?'
* '*Are you asking me if* I will need to do another course?'
* '*Can I just check, do you mean;* will I need to do another course?'
These questions can be answered using non-verbal communication. i.e. a nod of the head

Talking about different topics

EXAM INFORMATION: In **Part 1** you have to speak about **3 topics**. You may be asked a number of questions about each one. You need to practise **thinking quickly**. You also need to have a wide range of ideas so that you can change from one topic to the next.

1 Look at the following **Part 1 topics** and related questions. Write your own question for each one.

Topic 1: Jobs
1 What kind of work do you do?
2 Did you have to study before you started this job?
3 Is this a popular career choice in your country?
4 (Your idea) ....

Topic 2: Neighbours

1 Do you get on with your neighbours?
2 Do people in your country usually spend time socially with their neighbours?
3 Is it important to have neighbours?
4 (Your idea) ………………………….

Topic 3: Time

1 Do you always try to be on time for meetings and appointments?
2 Can you think of any situations where it is acceptable to be late?
3 How do your friends organise their time (i.e. Do they make a diary?)?
4 (Your idea) …………………………………………..

2 Work with a partner. Take it in turns to be the candidate and the examiner. Ask each other the questions from **exercise 1**.

3 Work with a partner. Take it in turns to be the candidate and the examiner. Ask each other the following **Part 1 questions.**

> ### EXAM TIP
> To give yourself a little more time to think about what you're going to say, you can repeat the question. You will have to change the pronoun.
> **Example: *What things do you have to do on the computer as part of your studies?***
> *'What things do I have to do on the computer as part of my course? Well…I probably use the computer quite a bit actually. A lot of my research is done on the internet, and, of course, most of my assignments have to be word-processed.'*

Topic 1: Studies

1 Are you attending school or university at the moment?
2 Is it important for you to study alone or in a group?
3 What kinds of things do you have to do as part of your studies that you need a computer for?
4 What would you like to study in the future?

Topic 2: Food

1 Do you think your diet is healthy?
2 Is traditional food popular in your country?
3 Do you think it is important that children are encouraged to eat healthily?

Topic 3: Animals

1 What is your favourite animal?
2 Did you keep animals as pets when you were a child?
3 Do you think children should be taught to look after animals?

IELTS Speaking Exam Guide

Explaining your likes and dislikes

In **Parts 1** and **2**, you have to say what you like and don't like. You need to:
- Learn some expressions to describe likes and dislikes.
- Give reasons for your preferences.

1 L3 Listen to 2 candidates answering the **Part 1 question** below. Make notes in the table as you listen.

a) What expressions are used to show likes and dislikes?
b) Does the speaker give any reasons for these likes or dislikes?
c) What tenses does **Speaker 1** use?

Question: *Do you like keeping flowers in your house?*

Speaker 1	Speaker 2
A Likes/Dislikes	**A Likes/Dislikes**
B Reasons	**B Reasons**

EXAM TIP

Don't repeat all the language in the question. You need to show the examiner your own vocabulary. Look back at **Chapter 1**, page 5, on how the IELTS Speaking test is assessed. You should have a wide range of vocabulary. Learn synonyms and parallel expressions i.e. words and phrases with similar meanings.

2 Read the following candidate answers to **Part 1** questions. Replace the underlined words with a synonym or parallel expression. An example has been done for you.

0 Question: Do you prefer eating at home or in restaurants?
Candidate: *I like <u>eating at home, but I prefer eating in restaurants.</u>*

> *Although I do sometimes enjoy <u>cooking in my own kitchen</u>, I think <u>eating out</u> is much better.*

1 Question: Which musical instrument would you like to start playing?
Candidate: I <u>would like to start playing</u> the piano.

_____

2 Question: What's the best thing about your home town?
Candidate: I think <u>the best thing about my home town</u> is the mountains around it.

_____

3 Question: What do you like about spending time with friends?
Candidate: <u>What I like about spending time with friends</u> is that we always have fun together.

_____

4 Study the expressions in the **Useful Language box** below. Use them when you speak and make them part of your speaking vocabulary. Keep adding any new expressions that you see and hear.

Useful Language: explaining likes and dislikes	
Likes	**Dislikes**
I really enjoy... One of the nicest things about ... is... I love... It makes me happy when... I'm very fond of...	I can't stand... I don't care that much for… One of my least favourite things is... I don't particularly like... I'm not really fond of...
Examples: *I love swimming.* *It makes me happy when my wife has dinner ready for me when I get home from work.*	**Examples:** *I can't stand driving in rush-hour traffic.* *I don't particularly like shopping.*

Part 1 topics

Look at the following possible **Part 1 topics**. Build vocabulary around these topics.

PART 1	
• Your spare time • Your studies • Your family / childhood • Food / restaurants / meals • Your hobbies / interests • Your country / home town • Your job • Your accommodation • Your room • An achievement you are proud of • The internet • Dreams • Animals • Newspapers/magazines • Neighbours/neighbourhoods • Letters and emails • The weather • Plants and flowers • Fruit and vegetables • Radio and television **KEEP ADDING TO THE LIST**	This is for you to add notes and questions you think an examiner may ask you. **Example: Your spare time** • What do you like to do in your free time? • Is free time important to you? • Do you prefer to be with your family or with your friends in your free time? **Example: Letters and emails** • Do you usually write letters, or emails? • When did you first send someone an email? • Do you think people will still use a pen and paper to write with in the future?

Chapter 3

PART 2
Talking about a topic

EXAM STRATEGY

In **Part 2** you will be given a topic card. On this card there are prompts to help you structure what you say. These prompts usually begin with a question word. i.e. 'What...Who...When...' Think of something to say about each one. You should try to use your own experiences and ideas.

You need to:

- Keep to the topic.
- Keep to the tense.
- Keep talking.

EXAM TIP

You are given 1 minute to make notes. Make these notes in English, not in your own language. You need to keep **thinking in English**.

---

1 Read the following **Part 2 topic card** and the **candidate's answer**. Underline the expressions that introduce each prompt.

Describe something you did that you are proud of.

You should say:
- What it was
- When you did it
- How it made you feel

You should also say what effect this achievement had on your life.

What it was	I'm going to talk about what I feel is probably my greatest achievement. I guess many people are proud of things having to do with their job ... maybe the amount of money they've made, but I suppose mine is more of an emotional achievement. I'm exceptionally proud of a competition I once took part in.
When you did it	It was about 5 years ago when I was still at university. I was studying engineering and there was a competition to see who could come up with a safer and more eco-friendly way of processing waste oil.
How it made you feel	After the competition, I remember feeling exhausted and relieved that it was all over. I did not win, which was a bit disappointing for me, but I was told by one of the judges that he really liked my ideas. What he said made me decide to keep some of my designs because I truly believed they would work. I'm really glad I did because, as it turns out, some of those processes that I designed then are now being used in the gas company I work for and that makes me very proud.

---

2 **L4** Listen to a candidate answering the following **Part 2 topic card** and answer the questions.

Describe a vehicle you would like to own.

You should say:
- What it is
- What it would look like
- Where you first saw it

You should also say if this vehicle is popular in your country.

---

1 Does the candidate use the prompts to help him?
2 Does he keep to the topic?
3 Is his answer long enough?
4 What did he do well?
5 How could he have improved his answer?

3 Work with a partner. Talk for at least one minute about the topic below. Check that your partner:

- Speaks for 1 minute.
- Keeps to the topic.
- Uses the correct verb tenses.

> Describe the place where you grew up.
>
> You should say:
>   - Where it was
>   - How long you lived there
>   - What you liked about it
>
> You should also say if you think this is a good place for children to grow up in.
> You need to speak for 1 to 2 minutes.

4 After you have spoken about the subject outlined on the topic card, you may be asked 1 or 2 follow-up questions. Look back at the topic cards in **questions 1** and **2**. Read the examples below and match the follow-up questions to each topic. Write **A** (Topic Card 1) or **B** (Topic Card 2) for **questions 1 - 4**.

1. Do you think you will buy this vehicle one day? **TOPIC** _____
2. Did you tell anyone else about what you did? **TOPIC** _____
3. Do you still feel the same way about this? **TOPIC** _____
4. Will this be expensive to buy? **TOPIC** _____

> ### EXAM TIP
> The follow-up questions are short answer questions. You do not have to give long answers. Answer the question with a brief reason / explanation, if necessary.
> **Example:** *Did you tell anyone else about what you did?*
> *'Yes, I told my family and they were obviously proud of me, especially my mother.'*

Pronunciation: Final consonants

Pronunciation mistakes can make you lose marks in the IELTS speaking test. If the examiner cannot understand what you are saying, it is difficult to get a good mark.

Remember:
Open your mouth (even if it feels unnatural). Do not speak through your teeth. Do not mumble. Make sure you have pronounced the ends of words or sentences. Do not swallow sounds. In particular, sounds like /s/, /z/, /d/, /k/, /n/ and /l/.

1 L5 Look at the words below. Fill in the gaps to make the words then put them in the correct place in the table according to their final consonant sound. Listen and check your answers.

1 import _ _ _ _	2 essen _ _ _ _	3 solu _ _ _ _	4 targ _ _ _
5 pub _ _ _	6 mult _ _ _ _	7 mov _ _	8 conven _ _ _ _ _
9 polic _ _ _	10 recy _ _ _ _	11 fut _ _ _	12 prop _ _ _
13 fundamen _ _ _	14 expl _ _ _	15 bic _ _ _ _	16 electr _ _ _ _
17 soci _ _ _ _	18 kno _ _	19 house _ _ _ _	20 insa _ _
			21 chan _ _ _

/s/	/z/	/d/	/k/	/n/	/l/

2 L6 Read the following **Part 2 topic card** and the **candidate's answer**. Practise reading it aloud and make sure the final consonants in the underlined words are pronounced. Add any new words to the table above. You can listen to the candidate's answer on the **Audio CD**.

> Describe a conversation you had recently that changed your way of thinking.
>
> You should say:
> - Who you spoke to
> - What you spoke about
> - What you liked about it
>
> You should also say if you think we communicate enough today.

Candidate's answer:

I remember one <u>conversation</u> in particular that <u>changed</u> my whole way of thinking about teaching <u>children</u>. It was a seminar I <u>attended</u> on the <u>importance</u> of teaching reading at <u>kindergarten level</u>. I spoke to a professor <u>afterwards</u> who said he thought it was <u>essential</u> children were taught to read as early as <u>possible</u>. He <u>moved</u> on to say that <u>teachers</u> should not be frightened of using <u>electronic books</u>. At first I thought this <u>sounded insane</u>, but then he said that children were extremely <u>sociable</u> at this age and <u>enjoyed</u> working together. Sometimes trying to force them to <u>read books</u> was <u>futile</u>. An easy <u>solution</u> was to allow them to <u>use computers,</u> and he said every primary school teacher today <u>knows the convenience</u> of using <u>these</u> in the <u>class</u>. I liked his <u>suggestion</u> that a long-term <u>solution</u> <u>required</u> an <u>expansion</u> into the <u>e-book</u> market. He finished by explaining that the government <u>needs</u> to start making <u>changes</u> to <u>education policies</u>. I think a <u>fundamental</u> problem is that we don't talk enough to each other today, so changes are difficult to make.

Part 2 topics

Look at the following possible **Part 2 topics**. Build vocabulary around these topics. Practise speaking about each one for 1 minute.

PART 2	
• A book you have read	• A plan you have made
• A person you admire	• A conversation you had recently that changed your way of thinking
• An achievement you're proud of	
• A toy you played with	• The type of weather you particularly like
• A party you attended	• Your school days
• A festival you've been to	• A television programme you watch
• A trip you've been on	• A piece of jewellery
• A film you've watched	• A garden/park you enjoy visiting
• A place you would like to visit	• An old building you remember
• Your favourite form of transport	• A course you are interested in
• Your favourite style of dress	• A family member you like to be with
• Your best friend	
• A sport you enjoy playing·	**KEEP ADDING TO THE LIST**
• A song you like listening to	

Chapter 4

PART 3
Introducing and organizing your opinions

EXAM INFORMATION:
In **Part 3** the examiner will say: *'I will now ask you some **GENERAL** questions.'* This means:
- Do not talk personally about yourself. You can use your personal experiences as a common example, but make sure you show this clearly in the language you use.

Example: *Most men in my country, like myself, enjoy being competitive, especially when it comes to sport. But I feel competition is important in many areas, such as business, so it is not exclusive to sport.*
- Talk about the world as a whole. Use global examples where possible.

Example: *I think the problem of traffic in cities is something that can be seen on an international scale in most major cities in the world, especially in countries like the UK and the USA.*

1 Structure what you say
1. Introduce your ideas with a **sentence starter**.
2. Support your main idea by adding extra information – an example or a reason.

Sentence starter
'Basically I feel that...'

Your main idea
'...it is not only the government's responsibility to solve the problems caused by heavy traffic.'

Extra Information (Reason)
The main reason behind my thinking this is that the general public has to accept the part they have to play. If we don't all work together, then the problem will probably never go away.'

2 Study the expressions in the **Useful Language Box** below.
Use them when you speak and make them part of your speaking vocabulary. Keep adding any new expressions that you see and hear.

Useful Language: structuring what you say

Sentence starters:
Introducing your ideas and opinions
- Basically, I feel that...
- If it were up to me I'd...
- I think ... should...
- My idea is that ... should...
- To me, what we need to be focusing on is...
- Personally speaking...
- It would seem to me that...
- Without a doubt I believe that...I truly believe that...
- I think most people feel / believe / think / accept that...
- I think you can look at this in a number of different ways...
- The thing we need to be looking at is...

Extra information to make your ideas clearer:
Giving reasons and examples
- One example that springs to mind us...
- Probably the best example I can think of is...
- In my country for instance...
- The reason I feel this way is because...
- There are several reasons why...
- One relatively easy way to do this is...
- Mainly, this is because...

Examples:
- Basically I feel that advertising can make people buy things.
- If it were up to me, I'd put a higher tax on big cars to try and encourage people to use public transport more.
- To me, what we need to be focusing on is how to make our economy stronger.
- I think governments should put more money into adult education.
- I think most people feel that women are just as capable of managing a company as men.
- I truly believe that we will find an alternative energy source in the future.
- One example that springs to mind is how winter can make you/someone feel more depressed because there is not much sunlight.
- There are several reasons why houses in hot countries are built this way. The first one is that they are designed to reflect heat.

3 Find appropriate phrases from the **Useful Language Box** to complete the following **Part 3 main ideas**. Use your own ideas to make your ideas clearer where necessary. The first one has been done as an example.

0 Children don't enjoy reading as much these days.	1 Advertising on the internet has more positive effects than negatives ones.	2 Families need to spend more time together.	3 Self-study is better than studying with a teacher.

> **0** **It would seem to me that** children don't enjoy reading as much these days. **In my country for instance,** most children prefer to watch television or play computer games. **To me, what we need to be focusing on is** educating parents and getting them to spend more time reading with their children. **One relatively easy way to do this is** by reading them bedtime stories.

Pronunciation: Pausing and Chunking

When we write, we use punctuation to make our writing easier to follow. When we speak we need to do the following to make our ideas easier to follow:

1 Breathe. When you are nervous, you may speak too quickly and forget to breathe regularly.
2 Pause in the right places.
3 Break up what you say into logical '**chunks**'.

> ### EXAM TIP
> If you pause in the wrong places, you could lose marks. You will sound unsure of what you mean and this will break your flow of ideas. You will also sound unnatural.

1 L7   Listen to a candidate answering the following **Part 3 question** and answer the questions.

Do you think the telephone is a popular form of communication?

    1 Does he pause in the right places?
    2 Is his answer easy to follow?
    3 Does he sound like he knows exactly what he is talking about?
    4 Does he sound natural?
    5 Would this candidate get a good mark for fluency?
    6 Would this candidate get a good mark for pronunciation?

> ### EXAM TIP
> Most English phrases end with nouns and verbs. Nouns and verbs have the most final-consonant clusters. i.e. *pick up those bags / I'd like to suggest*. When you pause at the end of a phrase:
> - You have more time to pronounce final consonants.
> - You give yourself a little time to think.
> - Your intonation and rhythm will sound better

2 L8 Read a candidate's answer to the following **Part 3** question and divide the sentences into logical chunks. Listen and check your answer.

> ## Do men and women like to read different types of books?
>
> Yes, I think it's in this way because the nature of women and men are very different so I think they choose different subjects and they have different tastes in reading. Yes for example I think women are very interested in reading novels that are based on love and affection. On the other hand I think men are very interested to read books for example the adventures and for example stories that are based on the travel of the person I mean biography for example and things like that.

3 L9 Listen to the candidate's answer again and answer the following questions.

1 Does she pause in the right places?

2 Is her answer easy to follow?

3 Does she sound like she knows exactly what she is talking about?

4 Does she sound natural?

5 Would this candidate get a good mark for fluency?

6 Would this candidate get a good mark for pronunciation?

7 What could the candidate do to improve her answer?

Pronunciation: Intonation

Intonation can show your attitudes and feelings. In English intonation, the voice usually goes up for a question and it falls to show completed statements.

> ### EXAM TIP
> English intonation is not monotone. It will be difficult to follow what you are saying if your voice does not rise and fall naturally

1 L10 Listen to a candidate answering the following Part 3 question and answer the questions.

Should boys and girls be given the same toys to play with?

1 Is his answer easy to follow?

2 Does he use intonation?

3 Does he sound natural?

5 Would this candidate get a good mark for fluency?

6 Would this candidate get a good mark for pronunciation?

2 L11 Now listen to another candidate answering the same question.

Predicting the future

EXAM INFORMATION:
In the IELTS Speaking test you may need to make predictions about future events or situations as in the exercise below.

1 L12 Listen to a candidate answering the question from the box above. Fill in the gaps as you listen.

> **Examiner:** *Do you think travelling will still be necessary in the future?*

Well, I think **1)**...................... that people will still need to travel in the future, especially people like businessmen and politicians. Of course, video-conferencing will **2)**................... mean that lots of meetings can be done from the office. Having said that, I'm **3)**...................... no future developments in technology will ever take away people's need to see new places first-hand and meet people face-to-face. The other thing is that families are also much further apart geographically today than they used to be. Different family members live and work abroad and I think this trend will **4)**................. continue in the future, which means people will have to travel to go and visit their families.

2 Put the expressions from **Exercise 3** into the table below.

I am sure	I am fairly sure	I am not sure

3 Add the following expressions to the table above.

1 I'm not actually sure if/whether…
2 There's no doubt in my mind that…
3 I would most definitely say that…
4 There is a good chance that…
5 I am absolutely convinced that…
6 It's impossible to say if/whether…
7 No-one really knows if…
8 There is a very real possibility that…
9 I don't really know if…
10 I truly believe that…
11 It could be/might be said that…

4 Work with a partner. Take it in turns to be the candidate and the examiner. Ask each other the following Part 3 questions. Use the expressions from the table to help you.

1 Where will most people live in the future, in towns or in the countryside?
2 Is it likely that we will still be reading books in paper form in the future?
3 Will people in your country have a healthier diet in 10 years time?
4 Do you think business men and women will still travel abroad for meetings in the future?
5 Do you think that people in the future will still want to learn about the history of their country?
6 What will be the most serious problem cities will have to face in the future?

5 L13 Listen to a candidate talking about his future study plans. What expressions does he use? Write **Y** for **Yes** or **N** for **No** for **Questions 1-8**

1 I aim to...   _____
2 I intend to...   _____
3 What I hope to develop from this is...   _____
4 My main goal is to...   _____
5 The main focus is to...   _____
6 I hope it'll help me to...   _____
7 The main purpose is to...   _____
8 What I hope to achieve from this is...   _____

6 Read the advertisement for a language course you are going to be taking. Talk about your plans and what you hope to achieve. Use the expressions from **Question 5** to help you.

ACADEMIC SPEAKING SKILLS COURSE

Length of course: 3 hours per week for 4 weeks.

Course Aims:

a) To learn how to effectively communicate in English at university.

b) To learn how to take part in discussions.

c) To get practice in expressing your ideas on a wide range of topics.

d) To build confidence in speaking in front of people.

Part 3 topics

Look at the following possible **Part 3** topics. Build vocabulary around these topics. Remember the vocabulary you use for **Part 3** speaking is formal. It is similar to the **writing style** you need for **Task 2**.

PART 3	
• The media.	• The importance of free time in our modern world.
• Journalism and if journalists have a responsibility to tell the truth.	• The importance of making plans and having goals.
• Advertising.	• Immigration.
• Music and culture.	• The importance of history and understanding your own country's history.
• The protection of wild animals.	• International history compared to local history.
• The environment.	• Studying and working abroad.
• Education.	• Private and public transport - advantages and disadvantages.
• Human relations / communication.	
• Population growth.	
• Social problems and issues.	
• Your government and some of their policies on health, education etc.	**KEEP ADDING TO THE LIST**
• Charities / International Aid.	
• The nature of human happiness.	
• The relationship between employers and employees.	

Chapter 5

PARTS 1, 2 and 3
Using Idiomatic language

1 Look at the two examples from a candidate's answer to the **Speaking Part 1** topic *Your Studies*. Which of the answers is better and why?

> **Speaker 1**
> I'm studying at the moment and I must confess that I find exams particularly stressful. Of course, I have good days and bad days like everyone else. Some days I'm so stressed out that I feel I want to throw in the towel. All I can do at such times is call it a day and get a good night's sleep! I usually find that things look different in the morning. It's like you have a fresh start and you can start studying again. At the end of the day, I know I have no choice; if I want to pass, I have to study!
>
> **Speaker 2**
> To tell you the truth, I'm a student and I really find it difficult to meet deadlines, especially essays. My mother said always I'm a bookworm! I usually find I have to work really hard, both day and night, but the early bird catches the worm. Of course I know I'll feel much better when I finally hand in my work because every coin has two sides.

> **EXAM TIP**
> You need to use idiomatic language in your speaking test, but you must make sure you use this language **accurately** and **appropriately**.

2 Add the idioms in the box to the sentences. Use a dictionary to check the meaning of any idioms you do not know. You may have to change the grammar.

A) to be part and parcel	B) to be on the same wavelength	C) in this day and age
D) one thing that strikes me about...	E) in the long run	F) a fresh start
G) to get the wrong end of the stick	H) get through the red tape	I) to go round in circles
J) (start) from scratch	K) to read between the lines	L) at the end of the day
M) to call it a day	N) to throw in the towel	O) to wear your heart on your sleeve
P) to call the shots	Q) the be-all and end-all	

1 I think you must have .... That wasn't what I meant at all. You completely misunderstood what I was saying.

2 My sister really .... She gets so emotional about every little thing.

3 I can't understand young people who think playing computer games is the .... of everything. I think there's more to life than sitting in front of a computer screen.

4 I honestly believe that the automobile industry should now completely forget about fossil fuels and .... by looking for alternative forms of energy.

5 It is not going to be easy for us to set up this new company. It's still a developing country so we are going to have to find ways to .... and deal with all the government regulations.

6 Although learning a new language is frustrating, I never considered .... because quitting is not an option for me.

7 .... it's hard to imagine our lives now without Facebook and Twitter.

8 Writing emails is certainly more time-consuming than talking on the phone, but .... , particularly in business, sometimes there has to be a written record.

9 Although recycling may initially cost a great deal of money, ... it will benefit the environment and could cut down on the detrimental effects caused by global warming.

10 My family and I are planning to move to Canada because we feel we really need ....

11 The student council meeting seemed to take forever. The discussion kept .... because some of the students could not agree, so it took about two hours before a decision was made.

12 My sister and I have always been really close. We have so much in common and I can instantly tell when she is upset because we ....

13 .... this whole issue of being in fashion is that young people are spending way too much money on clothes. It's almost becoming a negative obsession.

14 Making mistakes is .... of the language learning process but, it is only by correcting their mistakes that learners can move to the next stage.

15 Sometimes I feel it's better to .... than to struggle for hours with no results.

16 You mustn't take anything he says at face value because he is very good at hiding his feelings. The only way is to .... to find out what the truth is.

17 To a large extent, it's the bigger multi-national companies that are .... now, especially when it comes to influencing which products will dominate the international market. Smaller businesses just don't have enough resources or power to compete.

3 Answer the following **Speaking Part 3** questions with a partner. Use **idioms** from **Exercise 2** where appropriate.

1 (Topic: Fashion) Do you think people in your country will still be wearing traditional clothes in 10 years' time?

2 (Topic: Sport) Assess how sport competitions such as the Olympic Games can help relations between different countries to develop and improve.

3 (Topic: Aid) Compare the roles and influence of local and international charities.

4 (Topic: Childhood) Evaluate how much a happy childhood can influence a person's development as an adult.

5 (Topic: Competition) Do you think encouraging children to compete is positive or negative?

6 (Topic: Languages) Is it necessary to learn the culture of a country to learn the language?

Using collocations

> **STUDY TIP**
> It is important to learn which words usually go together to make natural-sounding English. A good English dictionary can help you with this.

4 Study the expressions in the **Useful Language Box** on the opposite page. Use them when you speak and make them part of your speaking vocabulary. Keep adding any new expressions that you see and hear.

Useful Language: collocations

Adverb + verb	**Verb + 'time'**	**Adjective + 'time'**
• I strongly believe that...	• spend time (with)	• free time
• I honestly believe that...	• waste time	• spare time
• I sincerely hope...	• save time	
• I totally support...	• make time	

Examples:
• I sincerely hope that people will still use libraries in the future.
• I totally support the idea of having more green spaces, like parks in cities.

Example:
• I spend most of my free time with my husband.
• Parents need to make more time to be with their children.

5 Find **2 adjectives** from the box that commonly **collocate** with each of the **nouns** below.

disruptive	relaxed	expensive	healthy	negative	anti-social

1 a)_____ b) _____ + lifestyle

2 a)_____ b) _____ + attitude

3 a)_____ b) _____ + behaviour

6 Which noun in each sentence does **NOT** collocate with the verb?

1	make	+	a) an effort	b) progress	c) an influence	d) a difference
2	save	+	a) energy	b) habits	c) space	d) lives
3	keep	+	a) attention	b) track	c) calm	d) a record
4	come	+	a) to a compromise	b) to a standstill	c) to a schedule	d) to an agreement
5	go	+	a) cooking	b) abroad	c) online	d) bankrupt
6	take	+	a) a break	b) a fine	c) an exam	d) notes

7 Read a candidate's answer to the following **Part 3 question** and **underline** the collocations.

How can people be encouraged to use public transport?

First of all, the most important thing for people nowadays is time. They don't want to actually waste their time so the public transport services should be very quick and run without any delays. I mean it's a real problem for me as a businessman when trains don't run on time. Public transport should also be easy to access. The other point is the expenses. I feel it should be cheap because if we are expected to use it, then it should be affordable. Maybe governments should pay some kind of subsidy to reduce the charges that the general public has to pay.

8 L14   Listen to a candidate answering the following **Part 1** question and answer the questions.

Do you like the place where you're living at the moment?

1   Does she use collocations?
2   Is her answer easy to follow?
3   Does her English sound natural?
4   Would this candidate get a good mark for fluency?
5   Would this candidate get a good mark for vocabulary?

Further practice: Parts 1, 2 and 3

EXAM INFORMATION:
Remember that you should:
- Answer the question directly.
- Develop your answer - give a short reason / example / explanation to support your idea.

For example:
Examiner: *Do you enjoy reading?*

'Oh yes, definitely; there's nothing I like better than to sit and read in the evenings just before I go to bed. I find it really relaxing and it also helps me sleep.'

1 Work with a partner. Ask each other the following **Part 1** questions.

Topic: Books
1 Do you enjoy reading? (Why/Why not?)
2 Has the internet changed the way you read?
3 Do you think we will still read books in the future?

Topic: Films
1 How often do you watch films?
2 Do you prefer to watch films on DVD or at the cinema? (Why?)
3 Do you think parents should control the kinds of films their children watch?

Topic: Mobile Phones
1 Are mobile phones popular in your country?
2 Is there anything you don't like about mobile phones? (Why?)
3 Do you think children should be allowed to have mobile phones?

Topic: Emails
1 How often do you write emails?
2 What sorts of things do you usually write about?
3 Do you think emails is a good way to communicate with others? (Why / Why not?)

2 L15 Listen to a candidate talking about films and answer the following questions.

I What *sentence starters* does he use?
2 What language does he use to show his likes / dislikes?

3 Look at the following **Part 2** topics. Work with a partner. Take it in turns to be the examiner and the candidate. Use the questions in **exercise I** to assess each other.

Examiner: I'd like you to speak about the following topic for I to 2 minutes. First, you have one minute to make notes and think about what you are going to say.

1 Describe your favourite TV programme you enjoyed watching when you were a child.

You should say:
- What it was about
- How often you watched it
- Why you enjoyed it

And you should also say whether people in your country regularly watch television

2 Describe a song that you enjoy listening to.

You should say:
- What it is
- When you like to listen to it
- Why you like this song

And you should also say why music is important to people.

3 Describe an advertisement you have seen or read recently that made you want to buy something.

You should say:
- Where you saw or read it
- Which product it was trying to sell
- What you liked about it

And you should also say whether or not advertising influences you.

4 Describe a photograph that you really like.

You should say:
- What it is
- Where it was taken
- Why you like it

And you should also say whether or not taking photographs is popular in your culture.

4 L16 Listen to a candidate talking about a song he enjoys listening to. Answer the following questions:

I What *sentence starters* does he use?
2 What collocations does he use?

5 L17 Read part of the candidate's answer and divide the sentences into logical chunks. Underline the main words that are stressed. Listen and check your answer.

> And one of the reasons I like this song is as I said before... the guitars. It's a rock-and-roll beat to the song, but it's also a... you know, it's a coming-of-age song. It's about young love. It reminds me of my working-class upbringing. It's about cars and the highway and young peoples' dreams. I think most people enjoy music for pretty much the same reasons as I do. Because music or songs usually tell a story or they inspire people or sometimes they bring back memories... or bring up dreams that you once had or dreams that you might still have. And I think that's very important to people. It kind of lightens the load ... And it's ... it's what music is all about, as far as I'm concerned.

6 Now ask each other the following **Part 3** questions that follow on from the **Part 2 topics** in **question 3**. Take it in turns to be the examiner and the candidate.

> **EXAM STRATEGY**
>
> Remember to expand your answers. Be careful with the tense. The verbs on the topic card will tell you if you should be speaking about the past, present or future.

Examiner: Now I'd like to ask you a few general questions about the topic you've just been speaking about.

Topic 1: TV programmes

1 Compare the kinds of TV programmes that children and adults usually enjoy watching.
2 Do you think that parents should control how much television their children watch?
3 Evaluate the effectiveness of television as a means of communicating the news compared with other media forms such as the internet and radio.

Topic 2: Music

1 Do people in your country prefer to listen to local or international music? (Why / Why not?)
2 Describe the importance of music in showing the culture of a country.
3 Evaluate the effect of technology (such as the internet) on music.

Topic 3: Advertising

1 Should companies be targeting children in their advertising campaigns?
2 Compare the use of the internet in advertising with other media forms such as television and radio.
3 Do you think advertisements should be censored? (Why / Why not?)

Topic 4: Photographs

1 Do you think photographs are important in helping us remember our past?
2 Why do you think people like to keep childhood photographs?
3 Should the private lives of famous people be respected by the media? (Why / Why not?)

6 L18   Listen to a candidate answering a **Part 3 question** on music.

Chapter 6

PARTS 1, 2 and 3
Test Advice

1 Read the test advice. Do you make any of the mistakes mentioned when you speak?

1 Listen carefully to the questions. Answer the questions directly.

2 In Parts 1 and 2, the examiner can only **REPEAT** the question. In Part 3 the examiner can **REPHRASE** the question.

3 Keep to the topic.

4 Do not give circular answers – an answer that keeps saying the same thing over and over again and does not get directly to the point.

5 Speak as clearly and as naturally as possible. Don't use expressions unless you know how to use them correctly. You will lose marks for unnatural English use. i.e. *step by step... / day by day... / as time passes by...*

6 Do **NOT** over-use words - *For example... / You know... / To some extent... / To tell you the truth...*

7 Remember in Part 3 that your answers need to be general. You are not talking about yourself (Parts 1 and 2). You are talking about people generally, the world as a whole

8 Do not give inappropriate scientific facts in Part 3. i.e. *It has been proven by scientists that... / According to the research of Professor...* You are being asked what **you think**, or to give **general information** about a topic.

9 Remember to breathe, pause and break up what you say into logical chunks.

10 It is your grammar and pronunciation mistakes that can affect your speaking grade. Make time to focus on these two areas.

2 Read the following candidate mistakes and match them to the advice given in exercise 1.

Examiner: Do you like shopping?

> To be honest, to tell you the truth, in my opinion I think it's really a little bit boring for me.

Examiner: Do you think a shortage of water will be a bigger problem than a shortage of oil in the future?

> Well yes definitely, I agree with this way of thinking. For example, in my city it is difficult even now to get fresh water. We have many problems with this. For example, sometimes there is not enough and we have drought. But with oil, for example, we have already started to use different fuels so I think this won't be such a big problem in the future. But when we look at water, it's a very different story and I think there could be a disaster for us because the water is not fresh enough to drink.

Examiner: What course would you like to do?

> I'm an engineer and I'm going for my job in Canada. That's why this IELTS course is very important for me. I need level 7. It's really necessary for me and my family. I did this test before, but my level was only 6. I hope you can help me.

Examiner: Should high-school teachers help their students set specific goals so that they can study better?

> You know, it is too important. My little brother he is very bad with this. He does not let his teacher help him at all so when he must study he does not at all. You know, he just plays on the computer. You know it is really very bad for him. My mother she tell him all the time to change but he not do it.

Examiner: Do you like swimming?

> Well to tell you the truth…. I am tremendously enthusiastic about swimming. It reminds me of my childhood. I was really keen on swimming when I was a child. I have sweet memories of my childhood, when I was swimming a lot. And also glorious, magical and hilarious moments of my childhood.

3 L19 Listen to the following candidate answering the **Part 2** topic below. Match the mistakes to the advice given in **exercise 1**.

---

1 I would like you to describe a famous sports person, who is not from your country, who you really admire.

You should say:
- Who this person is
- What you know about them
- Why you like them

And you should also say if this person is popular in your country.

Chapter 7

PARTS 1, 2 and 3
Test Practice

1 Practise this test with a partner. Take it in turns to be the examiner and the candidate. Read the test advice in **Chapter 6** again.

Part 1

Topic 1: Weekends

1 What did you do last weekend?

2 Do you prefer to spend the weekends with your family or friends?

3 What things do you like to do at the weekend?

Topic 2: Mobiles

1 How often do you use a mobile phone?

2 Have you ever had any problems using a mobile phone?

3 Do you think you will use a mobile more or less in the future?

Topic 3: Presents

1 Do you like receiving presents?

2 Who was the last person you gave a present to?

3 Is it better to give someone money rather than buy them a present? Why / Why not?

Part 2

Describe a business leader you respect and admire.

You should say:
- Who they are
- Where you first found out about them
- What you liked about them

You should also say if this person had an influence on you.
You need to speak for 1 to 2 minutes

Part 3

1 What qualities make someone a good leader?

2 Is there any difference between men and women as leaders?

3 Do leaders have a responsibility to behave in a certain way in public?

4 Are people born leaders or is this something they learn how to become?

L 20

2 Now listen to the practice test and make a note of any new expressions, idioms, collocations or sentence starters you hear.

L 20

3 Listen to the final two sections of Part 3 again and underline the key words that the speaker stresses.

Examiner: Do leaders have a responsibility to behave in a certain way in public?

Um I don't really think they have a responsibility to behave in a certain way, but I think they should behave in a certain way. Um because they have an immense platform on which they can sort of spread influence and so on and so many people look up to these people especially you know business leaders and so on. They're heroes to so many people. They should try and consider their position when they make decisions and you know .... understand that they are a role model for others, but I don't..I don't really think they should feel too much pressure to do that.

Examiner: Are people born leaders or is this something they learn how to become?

I think a lot of people would like to learn how to become leaders. Um I'm sure there's lots of people who do sort of business classes and things like that, wanting to be the next great business leader, but ultimately I think it is something you're born with unfortunately. You only have to look at a..a school playground, you'll see the natural leaders there riding around there from a very young age. Again it's difficult to see what it is that's making those people leaders, but I think you can inspire respect as you get older maybe by becoming an expert in a particular field, but whether that's the same as being a leader – I don't really think so I pretty much think it's something you're born with.

(A) Look at the pictures above. They show people on holiday in different places.
Think of as many different types of holiday as you can and write them down below.

Write down as many types of holiday as you can think of:

Romantic Holiday		
Short City Break		
Long Weekend		
Sun Holiday		
Package Holiday		

(B) What is your favourite type of holiday and why? Write your answer here, then cover it
and tell the class/a partner.

IELTS Speaking

(C) Link the following holiday-types (1) with the reasons for going on holiday (2).

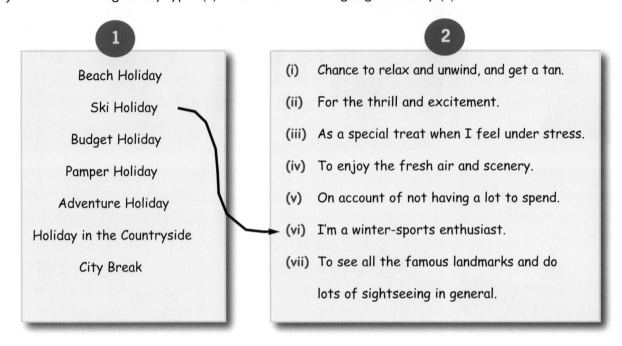

1

Beach Holiday

Ski Holiday

Budget Holiday

Pamper Holiday

Adventure Holiday

Holiday in the Countryside

City Break

2

(i)   Chance to relax and unwind, and get a tan.

(ii)   For the thrill and excitement.

(iii) As a special treat when I feel under stress.

(iv) To enjoy the fresh air and scenery.

(v)   On account of not having a lot to spend.

(vi) I'm a winter-sports enthusiast.

(vii) To see all the famous landmarks and do

       lots of sightseeing in general.

(D) Look at the following holiday activities. Which of them do you normally do when you go on holidays? Tick the boxes as appropriate.

(i) Go sightseeing and take pictures of famous landmarks. ❏

(ii) Dine out and sample the local cuisine. ❏

(iii) Sunbathe by the pool reading a book. ❏

(iv) Go on organised guided tours of places of interest. ❏

(v) Try to mingle with the locals and speak to them in their own language. ❏

(vi) Go on big shopping sprees and bring back lots of new clothes. ❏

(vii) Buy souvenirs for family and friends back home. ❏

(viii) Visit museums and art galleries. ❏

(ix) Spend most of the day relaxing in my hotel doing nothing. ❏

(x) Order room service and have breakfast in bed. ❏

(xi) Go to clubs and bars, party and have a wild time. ❏

(xii) Spend my time trying to pack in lots of things, and see as much as possible. ❏

(E) Compare your answers with a partner's. Decide if you would be suited to a holiday together. Be prepared to justify your decision.

(F) Rank the following holiday activities in order of preference, (1) being the activity you would most like to do on holidays and (10) being the one you would like to do least of all.

Activity	Ranking
(i) doing some general sightseeing	(1) _____
(ii) going on an excursion to a place of interest	(2) _____
(iii) taking a guided tour of a museum	(3) _____
(iv) dining out on traditional cuisine	(4) _____
(v) sunbathing by the pool	(5) _____
(vi) going on a city bus tour	(6) _____
(vii) getting some shopping therapy	(7) _____
(viii) going on a romantic riverboat cruise	(8) _____
(ix) going to the amusement park	(9) _____
(x) going trekking in the hills	(10) _____

(G) Look at the text and fill in the gaps with words from the box below.

My Perfect Holiday...

For me, the perfect holiday would have to be spent with my two best friends, George and Jeremy. We would go during spring, before the start of the tourist 1) _____ ; that way, the resorts would not be too crowded. The 2) _____ would be an easy choice; Spain every time. Why? Simply because it is the perfect combination - dependable weather, excellent 3) _____, friendly locals and lots to see and do. We would spend about a 4) _____ in Marbella, staying at a luxury beachfront hotel. Every morning we'd wake up to breakfast in bed. Then we'd go downstairs and outside onto the sandy beach, and in for a 5)_____ in the warm sea water to wake us up and refresh us for the day ahead. Next we'd go into town and do some 6) _____ , or go on a day trip of some sort. At lunchtime, we'd find a traditional restaurant and sample the local 7) _____. Each afternoon we were free, we'd do activities; maybe a bike ride around the olive groves or a pony ride through the nearby hills; you know... Then, in the early evening, we'd go back to the hotel and sit down on our deckchairs relaxing for a while on our balcony before going down to the hotel restaurant for some 8) _____ . Then we'd sit by the pool and read a book for a while until dinner was served. After dinner, we'd get dressed up for a night out and head into town to one of the popular nightclubs to party the night away. Each day would be similar to that with a blend of different types of activities. We'd have an absolute blast!

refreshments	sightseeing	delicacies	fortnight
dip	destination	season	cuisine

My Perfect Holiday

(H) Look at the passage *My Perfect Holiday...* again. In what order is the following information discussed?

Who the writer would go on holiday with.	1
What the writer would do on holiday.	____
Where the writer would go on holiday.	____
Where the writer would stay during his holiday.	____
When the writer would go on holiday.	____
Why the writer would go on holiday to this destination.	____

(I) Now it's your turn to tell us about your perfect holiday: what would it be like? Follow the steps below to answer the question.

Step 1 Make some notes

First, fill in the title to each section of your notes with an appropriate heading. Use the following titles and put them in the right order: *Who with, When, Where, Why, What (do)*

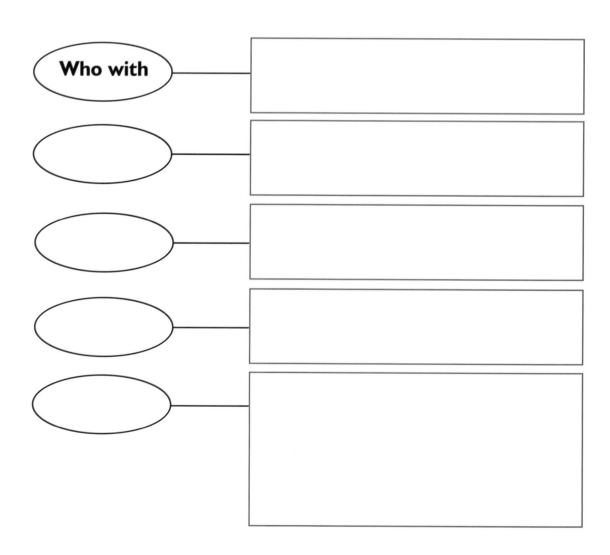

Step **2**   *Write your answer out in full.*

Step **3**   *Speak (put your written answer away and try to give a spoken answer referring back to your notes in Step 1 if you need to)*

(J) Talk about the following questions with a partner or as part of a class discussion.

- Which do you prefer; holidays in the city or holidays in the countryside?
- What is your favourite way of travelling long distances - by train, car etc.?
- Would you rather relax and take it easy when on holidays or try to see as many new things/ places as possible?
- Do you like to dine out when on holiday? What sorts of food do you eat?
- Do you prefer foreign or domestic holidays?
- What is your main reason for going on holiday, usually?
- Do you think a stay-at-home holiday can ever be as good as a proper holiday?
- Who do you usually go on holiday with? Do you prefer to holiday with friends or family?

Part 1 of the Speaking exam is a short introductory conversation lasting 4-5 minutes.
It tests your ability to talk about personal experiences and interests.
You must answer questions about everyday topics, talking about aspects of your life such as your family and friends,
home, studies, work, leisure activities, likes and dislikes etc.
You should answer each question appropriately, typically in one or two sentences.

(K) Look at these questions and answers. For each question, there are two answer choices. Choose the correct
alternative.

(1)   How long have you been learning English?
Since 8 years. / For eight years.

(2)   Do a lot of people in your country speak English?
Yes, they do. / Yes, they are.

(3)   Do you like learning English?
Yes, they are very interesting. / Yes, it is very interesting.

(4)   Have you studied any other languages?
Until I was 15, I have studied French. / Until I was 15, I studied French.

(5)   What advice would you give to a friend who wanted to start learning a language?
Go to the class. / Go to a class.

(L) The correct answers in (K) are a little too short. Select an appropriate sentence from the options below to
add to each answer.

(a) I start in sixth class if I remember correctly, when I was just 10 years old.   _____

(b) I would say close to half the adults where I come from are fairly fluent.   _____

(c) I used to very much enjoy studying the French.   _____

(d) And not just interesting; it's essential really, too; I mean, it opens up the
whole of the internet to me, for example.   _____

(e) Yes, the class is the very best way to learn a new language.   _____

(f) The fact is, every student needs support and guidance, and I always
find the advice and support of my teacher and fellow students vital.   _____

(g) A lot of you speak many languages such as French and German, too.   _____

(h) I started when I was 9 and a half I think, but it's so long ago I can barely remember!   (1)

(i) I find I am interested in any other subject I study.   _____

(j) I had to give it up though; I just had too much on to cope with another subject.   _____

Exam Focus: Part I  You must...

1 **Talk about some aspects of your personal life.**

2 **Answer the questions appropriately (usually 1-2 sentences).**

This part normally lasts 4-5 minutes.

Speaking Test 1

Part 1

The examiner will ask you some questions about yourself.

Let's talk about travel.
How often do you go on holiday?
Where did you go most recently?
Who do you normally go on holiday with?
Do you have a favourite place to go on holiday?
What do you normally pack in your suitcase when you go away?

The examiner will then ask you some questions about one or two other topics. See the example below.

Now let's talk about your family.
Do you come from a big or small family?
What do your parents do for a living?
How do you get along with the rest of your family?
Do you share the same interests as the other members of your family?
Is it good being the middle (an only / the eldest / the youngest etc.) child?

Part 2

The examiner will give you a topic on a card like the one below and ask you to talk about it for one to two minutes. Before you talk you have one minute to think about what you want to say. The examiner will give you some paper and a pencil so you can make notes if you want to.

> Describe your perfect holiday.
> You should say:
>   • where you would go and who you would go with
>   • where you would stay
>   • what you would do
> and explain why it would be the perfect holiday.

The examiner may ask you one or two more related questions when you have finished, like those given in the example below.

Do you prefer active holidays or holidays where you get to relax?
*Are there any countries you would **not** like to visit?*   *What was your worst holiday experience?*

Part 3

The examiner will ask you some more general questions which follow on from the topic in Part 2.

What are the benefits of holidaying in a foreign country?
What sorts of problems can people experience when they are abroad?
Do you think foreign holidays are affordable to everyone these days?
Is flying a safe way to travel?
Do you think people have enough time off work?
Why do some people come back from holidays more stressed than when they left?
What safety issues do you have to think about when you go away on holiday?

Unit 2 Life in the 21st Century

(A) Look at the pictures below. How important are these items to our lives today? Discuss with a partner, then rank the items in terms of importance from 1 to 5.

(i)　(ii)　(iii)　(iv)　(v)

Ranking: 1: _____   2: _____   3: _____   4: _____   5: _____

(B) You will hear five extracts. Each extract relates to one of the items pictured above. Match the extracts to the pictures. Write the correct picture (i-v) in the space provided.

Extract 1 _____　　Extract 2 _____　　Extract 3 _____

Extract 4 _____　　Extract 5 _____

(C) Soon, you are going to prepare a short speaking exercise. But first you will read some more about Part 2 of the Speaking test and ways to prepare for it on the pages which follow. After you have finished reading about Part 2, you will be asked to answer the following question, speaking continuously for about two minutes. The question is: *Which one of the items in the pictures above is most useful to you?* In your answer you should say:

- what the item is
- how often you use it
- what you use it for
- why it is so useful to you

Exam Focus: Part 2

In Part 2 of the exam, you will be asked to give a short talk for about two minutes. You will be tested on your ability to organise your ideas and speak fluently.

You will have to prepare and talk about a topic given to you during the test by the examiner.

Here is an example Part 2 task (you will be given a similar task-card by the examiner):

Remember you should provide each of the pieces of information asked for.

Describe a website you like to visit a lot.

You should say:

• the name of the website
• how often you visit the website
• what the website is for/about
• what you do/look at on the website

and explain why you like it.

Read the topic and make sure you understand it.

This part normally lasts 3 minutes.

You must...

1. **Read the task.**

2. **Make notes on each of the parts (approx. I minute).**

3. **Talk about the topic, answering the questions on the card.**

4. **Stop talking (after about 2 min.) when the examiner tells you to.**

5. **Answer some follow-up questions.**

In this book, you will learn a step-by-step strategy for practising how to talk continuously for up to two minutes that will help you to build up your confidence so that you are ready for the task come exam day.

We start off by making notes - a kind of brainstorm which gets you thinking of ideas. Then we write our answer down in full. Next, we put the written answer to one side (without memorising it) and we attempt to talk for as long as we can about the subject with the help of our notes.

At first, it may be hard for you to do this, but as you practise, you will find yourself having more and more to say. Eventually, you will become a lot more fluent and you will rely far less, if at all, on your notes. What's more, your confidence in your ability to express yourself will improve.

The note-making and writing will train your brain to think about and organise your answers logically. This will provide you with a starting point for your speaking and give you more to say. Eventually, you will become so good at organising your thoughts that you will no longer be reliant on the notes and you will be able to put your thoughts together more or less as you speak. **YOU MUST NEVER TRY TO MEMORISE YOUR WRITTEN ANSWERS THOUGH** as this defeats the purpose of the exercise. *See the next page for more.*

IELTS Speaking

EXAMPLE:

> Describe a website you like to visit a lot.
>
> You should say:
>
> - the name of the website
> - how often you visit the website
> - what the website is for/about
> - what you do/look at on the website
> - and explain why you like it.

Step 1 *Make notes*

Name - Facebook

Visit - Twice a day (at least)

For - friends to keep in contact

Do - send messages to friends, look at friends' news; post pictures and videos I like; comment on friends' pictures and videos; write on friends' walls (wall is the place where all a friend's news is seen); comment on friends' pictures and videos; say what I am doing; see what friends are doing; post links to other websites, 'like' different things (to like something you press a 'like' button on the website; means you are a fan of it...) - can 'like' music, pages, programmes, people; all sorts of things...; also able to play games - Facebook has lots of games apps

Why I like it - a great way to keep in touch with people - literally everyone; close friends, family, friends who live far away, work colleagues etc.; can find out all their news and keep them up to date with what you're doing as well, plus you're in control - get to decide who sees your pictures and posts and you can even set up groups for different kinds of friends; this means you don't have to share everything with all your friends; can choose who sees what; also love the games, so much fun, like Farmville - can create my own little online farm and become a virtual farmer and even build up a virtual farming community!! There's so much you can do...

Step ② *Write Answer*

> **Always introduce the topic.**

(a) A <u>website I love to visit is</u> Facebook - you probably know that one! Most people do since it's one of the most visited sites in the world.

(b) <u>I visit it at least twice a</u> day, and often more - it's so addictive that

(c) sometimes I stay on it for hours actually! <u>Facebook is basically designed</u> for people who want to keep in touch with their friends. It's a bit like a chat site, I suppose - but that's not doing it justice;

(d) the site's amazing really. <u>I mean, I can use it for</u> so many different types of things; I can message my friends on it, <u>check out their news</u> and see <u>what they're up to</u>, post pictures and videos that I like onto my page and see the ones friends have posted, too. I can write on my friends' walls - a wall is sort of like a webpage where all a friend's news and updates can be seen. I can comment on my friends' pictures and photos, too, and they can comment on mine - so long as they don't say anything nasty! Then again, if they did, I could just 'unfriend' them, so it wouldn't matter anyway! I can say what I'm doing by updating my status, see what friends are doing, and 'like' lots of different things. 'Liking' is when you want to show your appreciation for something or tell everyone that you are a fan of it. Basically, if you like something, you just click the 'like' button on the page. You can like music, pages, videos, updates; all sorts of things

(e) really... You can also play games on Facebook - <u>it has tons of great</u> apps. As for why I like it; it couldn't be simpler really; it's just the best site on the net! It is a brilliant way of keeping in touch with people, from family to close friends to faraway friends or even just acquaintances. You can find out all their news and keep them up to date with what you are up to, too. Another great thing is that you control what people can see and you decide who to share your news and updates with. Oh, and did I mention the games? I love them all, but especially Farmville; you can create your own little farm and become a virtual farmer - and even build a virtual farming community!! There's so much you can do I could go on all day!

> Notice how the register isn't that formal - in Parts 1 and 2 you don't have to use very formal language.

> Using language that sounds authentic, like phrasal verbs and lots of idioms will impress the examiner - provided they are used in the right way!

> Just as when writing, it is very important to use linking words and phrases to bring your talk together and to help your ideas flow smoothly.

> **Remember:** you should answer all the questions on the prompt card in order to maximise your score. Here, each new point answered is marked with a letter, (a), (b), (c), (d) or (e), and underlined.

Step ③ *Speak!*

This step is very simple (and yet perhaps the most difficult of all); now that you have structured your thoughts and put them into a logical order, you should have plenty to say. Put away the written answer, and, using only your notes to help you, try to speak for as long as you can about the subject. Allow the ideas to flow from your mouth and don't worry if you can't speak as well as you've written; just try your best to be fluent - keep going! - and natural-sounding. With practice, your confidence will improve as will the manner in which your express your ideas.

IELTS Speaking

Remember the steps in our practice method...

1   **Make notes on each of the separate parts of the task.**

2   **Convert your notes into a written answer.**

3   **Try to speak for about two minutes using only your notes to help you.**

Now, let's look at question C again.

(C) *Which one of the items in the pictures on page 38, is most useful to you?*

In your answer you should say:

- what the item is
- how often you use it
- what you use it for

And why it is useful to you.

Complete your answer by following the steps below.

Step **1**   *Make Notes*

_____

_____

_____

_____

_____

Step **2**   *Write Answer*

_____

_____

_____

_____

_____

_____

_____

_____

Step **3**   *Speak!*

(D) Look at the pictures below. They show two different families. Picture (i) was taken in the 1980s and Picture (ii) was taken in the 2000s.

(i)

(ii)

Discuss the following questions with a partner:

(a) In what ways might life have been different for the family in Picture (i) in the 1980s compared with life for the family in Picture (ii) in the 2000s?

(b) Do you think the children would have done the same things, played the same games, had the same hobbies, worn the same clothes, behaved in the same way, listened to the same music etc.?

(c) What have been the big changes in our lifestyle today compared with 20 or 30 years ago?

(E) Listen to the recording of a teenager talking about her life, and fill in the gaps in the transcript below using the words that you hear. Write **NO MORE THAN THREE WORDS** in each gap.

I was really excited today when I heard the news my parents had; you'll never guess what; I'm going to _____ !! Isn't that so cool? I mean, I've never been to _____ before in my life and neither have any of my friends. And we're taking _____ over from Pembroke port in Wales. It's a four-hour journey, I think. Can you believe it? The ferry! None of my friends have been on one of those yet either. I'm going to _____ to my aunt in Dublin to tell her I'm coming over to see her. I wonder what she'll look like in person; I've only ever seen the photos of her that she's sent _____ . We don't even get to talk that much really; well, every Sunday night _____ , but that's only for about five minutes - phone calls are _____ , you know... Anyway, now we'll finally get to meet. I'm going to bring my camera and take as many shots as I can. I bought five _____ yesterday; my camera will be click, click, click!

Then discuss the questions below with a partner:

- When do you think this recording of a teenage girl was made - in the 80s or today?
- What evidence is there to support your opinion?

IELTS Speaking

(F) Sort the phrases in the box below into *ones that probably relate to life in the 1980s* (A) and *ones that probably relate to life today* (B).

many stay-at-home mothers	families play board games at night
young children text each other	domestic holidays dominate
most school-leavers go straight into the workplace	the number of college graduates is very high
people do their banking online	young people are very confident and loud
discipline in schools is good	it is cool to smoke
the TV listings give 400 different channels	most music sales are downloads
televisions are expensive and there is only one in every house	international flights are very cheap
houses are affordable for first-time buyers	cigarette advertising is banned
most people are married by age 25	few people are computer literate
most people go on foreign holidays	distance learning courses are very popular
there are many jobs in I.T.	telephone boxes are used very regularly

A (1980s)	B (today)

Add your own points...

Add your own points...

(G) Use the three-step method (note-taking ... written answer ... spoken answer) to do the following task. Once you have finished your written answer, give your talk to the class.

> Describe a typical day in your life.
> You should say:
> - at what time you get up
> - what you normally do in the morning
> - what you normally do in the afternoon and evening
>
> and give examples of ways you like to relax after a busy day.

Make Notes

Write Answer

Speak

(H) Now pair off with another student and ask each other these follow-up questions:

(i) Do you think your daily routine would be very different if you were actually living in the year 1981?

(ii) What sorts of activities do people do today which might not have been so popular 20 or 30 years ago?

(iii) What aspects of life today would you miss the most if you were taken back in time to the 1980s and left there, do you think?

(iv) Do you think you have an easier life than people your age did in the past?

(I) Here are some further Part 2 questions for you to practise in your own time.

Describe your favourite piece of technology.
You should say:

- what it is

- how expensive it is and where you can buy it

- what it does

and why you like it so much.

1

Follow-up Questions:

- What piece of technology do you think, would be hardest to live without?

- What are the most popular technological devices with young people nowadays?

Describe what life was like when you were a young child.
You should say:

- where you lived and what your daily routine was like

- how you felt about school

- what you used to do in your free time

and explain how your life is different now.

2

Follow-up Questions:

- Did you find life easier when you were very young?

- Do you agree with people who say our school days are the best of our lives?

Speaking Test 2

PART 1

The examiner will ask you some questions about yourself.

> **Let's talk about your home town.**
> Where do you come from?
> What is it like where you live?
> Do you like living there?
> Have you always lived in the same place?
> What is there to do near where you live?

The examiner will then ask you some questions about one or two other topics. See the example below.

> **Now let's talk about learning languages.**
> How long have you been learning English?
> Do most people in your country learn English?
> Have you studied any other languages? Which language do you find easiest?
> Do you think it is important to learn English?
> What advice would you give to someone who wants to start learning a foreign language?

PART 2

The examiner will give you a topic on a card like the one below and ask you to talk about it for one to two minutes. Before you talk you have one minute to think about what you want to say. The examiner will give you some paper and a pencil so you can make notes if you want to.

> Describe a website you like to visit a lot.
>
> > You should say:
> > - the name of the website and how often you visit it
> > - what the website is for/about
> > - what you do/look at on the website
> and explain why you like it.

The examiner may ask you one or two more related questions when you have finished, like those given in the example below.

> Do you spend a lot of time online?
> Apart from looking at websites, what else do you do online?
> Do you think the internet is very useful, or not really?

PART 3

The examiner will ask you some more general questions which follow on from the topic in Part 2.

> Is surfing the internet more or less popular today than it used to be, in your opinion?
> What would you say are the main reasons people use the internet?
> Do you agree with people who say the internet is addictive?
> Do you think it is healthy when people spend a lot of time online?
> What are the dangers people using the internet face?
> The internet is very important to the way we live our lives in the 21st century. Do you agree?
> Are we influenced by what we read and see on the internet?
> Do you think the internet is a reliable source of information?

Unit 3 Art and Culture

Architecture

Sculpture

Performance Art

Dance

Painting

(A) Look at the pictures above and talk about the questions with a partner or as part of a class discussion.

- Which of these art forms do you find most appealing and why?
- What other forms of art can you think of?
- Would you describe yourself as an artistic person?
- What kinds of qualities do you need to possess to be an artist?
- Is creating art just a waste of time that could be better spent?
- Why are some forms of art more popular than others?

PART 3

Questions (iv), (v) and **(vi)** are all examples of **Speaking Part 3** questions. Look at the style of questioning; you are not being asked about yourself; you are being asked about general and abstract ideas. Look at the language used; in Part 3, there is a shift to a more formal register.

Part 3 is testing your ability to analyse and discuss ideas in more detail.

In **Part 3** you are required to answer questions that **relate** to the topic discussed in **Part 2**. You must offer your opinions and give reasons for them.

Exam Focus: Part 3   You must...

1 **Answer general questions related to the topic in Part 2.**

2 **Make sure to justify (give reasons for) your opinions.**

This part normally lasts 4-5 minutes.

Giving Opinions

(B) Correct the mistakes in the following expressions used for giving your opinion.

1. From my view, ...	In my view _____
2. So far as I am concerned, ...	_____
3. I completely agree the idea that...	_____
4. A way I see it...	_____
5. From the point of my view, ...	_____
6. I am absolutely agree that...	_____
7. To my way to think, ...	_____
8. Let me explain the reasons about my opinion;	_____

Talking about the future

(C) Put the words in the right order to reveal ways to express your confidence in what will happen in the future. Then group the phrases into **columns A** and **B** of the table as in the example.

1. that / I / imagine / cannot	I cannot imagine that... _____
2. doubt / highly / I / that	_____
3. not / at / convinced / all / I / am / that	_____
4. I / total / have / confidence / that	_____
5. fairly / certain / I / am / that	_____
6. seems / likely / that / it / me / to	_____
7. improbable / it / that / seems / highly	_____
8. very / sceptical / whether / about / am / I	_____
9. I / that / quite / sure / am	_____
10. say / would / that / I	_____

A (Confident)	B (Not confident)
	I cannot imagine that...

(D) Listen carefully to the Recording and decide whether each statement is **True** or **False**. 🎧

1. The student implies that music appeals to more people than theatre.   **T**

2. The student says most people prefer forms of entertainment which force them to think a lot.   _____

3. The student considers people who like art to be intellectuals.   _____

4. The student considers art to be something that few people can truly appreciate.   _____

5. The student is rather sceptical about the value of art critics' views.   _____

6. The student expects people to read fewer books in the future.   _____

7. The student thinks that the quality of films produced will improve in the future.   _____

8. The student sees a big future for virtual theatre.   _____

9. The student regards dance and music as forms of entertainment that are sure to remain popular.   _____

10. From his various answers, we can infer that the student thinks that theatre performances provide poor value for money.   _____

(E) Cover the questions below and listen to the Recording. Once the Recording is finished, look at the questions and answer them in your own words. 🎧

1. What does the student suggest as a way of getting more people interested in Art?

_____

_____

_____

_____

2. What do **you** think of her suggestion?

_____

_____

_____

3. The student mentions children, but what about adults?
   What would **you** suggest to get more adults interested in Art?

_____

_____

_____

_____

_____

4. Now talk about your answers with a partner or as part of a class discussion.

(F) Answer the following questions. Where relevant, try to use the phrases you have learnt to express your opinion and talk about the future. Write your answers down first to help you organise your thoughts. Then put your written answers to one side and discuss the questions orally with a partner or as part of a class discussion.

1. 'Some paintings really are worth millions of pounds.' Do you agree?

_____

_____

_____

_____

_____

2. Do you think people are born with artistic talent or can it be learnt?

_____

_____

_____

_____

_____

3. 'Most young people regard museums and art galleries as boring places.' Do you agree?

_____

_____

_____

_____

_____

4. Would you say it is easy to become a success in the art world?

_____

_____

_____

_____

_____

5. What perceptions, good and bad, do people generally have about artists?

_____

_____

_____

_____

_____

(G) Look at the passage about London below. Some words are missing from the text. Select the appropriate word from the box to fill each gap.

minority	cosmopolitan	roots
inhabitants	originate	diverse

Today, London is one of the most ethnically **(a)** _____ cities in the world. Only about half of its **(b)** _____ are white British, while around 13% **(c)** _____ from Asia. There is a large Indian representation also evident in the city, thought to account for approximately 6.5% of the population. The contingent of Londoners who have African **(d)** _____ is also rising - at a faster rate, in fact, than that of any other ethnic **(e)** _____ , with estimates putting the Africa-descendent share of the population at 5.5%. Across the city, there are over three hundred different languages spoken and it is thought that there are about 50 separate non-indigenous communities with a population totalling at least 10,000. London is truly **(f)** _____ .

(H) Now read the passage again and discuss these questions, either with a partner or as a class:

- What might be the benefits of living in a multicultural city like London?
- What problems can people living in places where lots of different cultures mix sometimes face?
- Would your home town be regarded as multicultural?
- Do you think there is a danger that, when lots of people from different backgrounds come to live in a place, the old traditions of that place might be lost?
- Is it important to learn about other cultures? Why?

(I) Listen to the Recording. Which question **(i-v)** from section **(H)** is the student answering? How do you know?

(J) In the recording you just heard, the following words or phrases were used. Match them to their meanings.

Word / Phrase	Meaning
tolerance ____	(i) The quality of being fair and objective and open to people behaving differently to the way you do.
discrimination ____	(ii) A blend or mix of different things.
prejudice ____	(iii) A general image you have (usually negative) which applies to a whole ethnic group.
stereotype ____	(iv) An unfavourable feeling or opinion about something, formed before you know enough to really judge the situation properly.
fusion ____	(v) Treating someone unfairly based on their appearance, background etc.

(K) Look at the passage about Saint Patrick's Day below. Some words are missing from the text. Select the appropriate word from the box to fill each gap.

| celebrations | floats | parade | fireworks |
| festival | fancy dress | national | venues |

Saint Patrick's Day

Saint Patrick's Day (17th March) is a **1)** _____ holiday in Ireland and a huge celebration around the world. Each year the St. Patrick's Day **2)** _____ is held over the weekend closest to March 17th. Events take place in **3)** _____ all over Ireland's capital city, Dublin. There are concerts, street theatre performances, parties and dances, and live traditional music can be enjoyed in virtually every city-centre bar. On the day itself, there is a huge **4)** _____ through the streets of Dublin, involving performers and marching bands from throughout Ireland and all around the world. Many people taking part in the parade wear **5)** _____ ; all sorts of colourful costumes are on display. The **6)** _____ which parade around the city are equally colourful and imaginatively designed. Hundreds of thousands of people line the streets to watch the parade and the festival culminates with a huge **7)** _____ display on Saint Patrick's Night. Similar parades and festivities take place throughout the country. In fact, the tradition of celebrating Saint Patrick's has spread far and wide beyond the shores of Ireland, too; parades and **8)** _____ are held every year in London, New York, Boston, Sydney, Tokyo and in many of the other major cities around the world. The river running through the city of New York, the Hudson, turns green to mark the occasion, as do some of the world's most famous landmarks, such as the London Eye, Niagara Falls, the Empire State Building and the Burj Al Arab.

(L) Now read the passage again and discuss these questions, either with a partner or as a class:

(i) Why do you think some festivals, like Saint Patrick's Day or the Rio Carnival, become popular all around the world?

(ii) Do you think national celebrations like Saint Patrick's Day are a good thing? Why / why not?

(M)

Think about a celebration in your country which is very popular.

- Make some notes about it.
- Write a paragraph describing the celebration.
- Write an answer to the question:
  What are the positive (or negative) effects of the celebration you described?

Notes:

Write a paragraph describing the celebration:

_____
_____
_____
_____
_____
_____
_____

What are the positive (or negative) effects of the celebration you described?

_____
_____
_____

(K) Now speak to the class for about two minutes about the celebration you described (referring only to your notes and not your written answer).

Speaking Test 3

PART 1

The examiner will ask you some questions about yourself.

Let's talk about your hobbies and interests.
What do you like to do in your free time?
Do you enjoy playing sports?
What types of music do you like?
Do you play any musical instruments?
What sport or hobby do you think you might like to try in the future?

The examiner will then ask you some questions about one or two other topics. See the example below.

Now let's talk about your likes and dislikes.
Do you like to eat food from other countries?
What's your favourite foreign dish?
Which do you prefer; holidays in foreign countries or holidays in your own country?
What do you like most about your country?
Do you prefer going to the theatre to see a play or watching movies at the cinema?

PART 2

The examiner will give you a topic on a card like the one below and ask you to talk about it for one to two minutes. Before you talk you have one minute to think about what you want to say. The examiner will give you some paper and a pencil so you can make notes if you want to.

> Describe a traditional celebration you like.
>
> You should say:
> - what the celebration is
> - who you normally celebrate with and where you normally celebrate
> - what you do during the celebration
>   and explain why you like it.

The examiner may ask you one or two more related questions when you have finished, like those given in the example below.

Do you prefer to celebrate important occasions with small or large groups of people?

Are you familiar with any celebrations from other countries?

What sorts of food do you normally find at celebrations you've been to?

PART 3

The examiner will ask you some more general questions which follow on from the topic in Part 2.

Why are national celebrations important?

Do you think celebrations like Christmas are too commercial?

Is it important to learn about the culture and customs of other countries? Why / why not?

Do you think everyone will end up celebrating the same things eventually?

Are some celebrations better than others? Explain.

What do you think accounts for the popularity of celebrations like Christmas and Halloween?

Why do you think food plays a big role in most celebrations?

Is it important to preserve tradition or should we move with the times more?

Longleat

Longleat, Somerset's famous safari park, is the oldest attraction of its kind in the world outside of Africa. Since 1966, visitors have been able to take their cars for a drive through enclosures full of lions, tigers, wolves and other magnificent apex predators, not to mention huge white rhinos and elephants (well, the resident elephant, Anne, at least). It is a magical - and at times hair-raising experience for little and big kids alike. And what makes a trip there even more worthwhile is the knowledge that your entrance fee is supporting an organisation that is committed to animal welfare. The animals at Longleat are not kept in tiny enclosures; there are no depressed faces looking out through the iron bars of a cramped cage; there is no pacing up and down the same three-metre-long area of grass all day; at Longleat, the animals come first and their needs are put before even the desire of visitors to get value for their money. If Anne the Elephant wants to go into her shelter, she is free to do so any time; if the gorilla wants to retreat to his sofa and watch some satellite T.V. (I kid you not!), then that's his prerogative - visitors just have to accept this. But even if you miss a few encounters on your drive around the park, you seldom go away disappointed because the animals that you do see reward you in full - like this handsome lion here. I must admit, though, that the hair on the back of my neck was standing up pretty straight when I first caught sight of the king of the jungle approaching from behind. Now that's an image I never thought I'd see out of my rear-view mirror - yikes!!

(A) Read the text above and then discuss these questions with a partner or as a class.

1. From what you have read about Longleat, do you approve of what it does?
2. Look at the picture top-left of the page; how would you feel if you were the driver of this car?
3. Would you like to visit Longleat? Why / why not?
4. Have you ever been to a similar park?
5. Do you think it is fair to keep animals in captivity in a place like Longleat?
6. How is a safari park different to a zoo?
7. What are the benefits of keeping animals in safari parks and zoos?
8. Would you consider yourself an animal lover?
9. Do we have a responsibility to look after the planet's animal life?
10. Can you think of any dangers that might be associated with a place like Longleat - for the animals or the visitors?

Keeping Animals in Captivity

(B) Read the passage FOR and the passage AGAINST keeping animals in captivity and fill each gap with a word/phrase from the box at the bottom of the page. Use each word/phrase **once** only.

For

Keeping animals in captivity is extremely important for many reasons. Zoos, for example, perform a vital function in helping to (a) _____ children and allowing them to (b) _____ the wonders of nature. They teach children to (c) _____ animals. But not only this, they are also important for (d) _____ and (e) _____ purposes. Zoos protect and study populations of species that are (f) _____ in the wild. Without this contribution, such species could become (g) _____ . As for pets, well, what needs to be said really? They are our constant (h) _____ and our best friends. They keep us company, protect us, love us and appreciate us; in some cases, the bond between pet and owner is stronger than the owner's relationship with any other human being. And another thing; people like to bash animal testing, but the truth is that without it we wouldn't be able to find (i) _____ for some of the most deadly diseases. Animal testing is, unfortunately, a necessary evil; in order to advance science and medicine, it is a practice that must be employed. But most animals in captivity are not subject to lab tests anyway. In fact, the vast majority benefit from their relationship with humans - and goodness knows, we benefit from our relationship with them, too. Having animals around makes us more (j) _____ and, well, more human actually.

Against

Keeping animals in captivity is a form of (i) _____cruelty_____ whatever way you look at it and there are countless examples of this. Take the circus, where we make animals perform tricks for our (ii) _____ and whip them when they do not. If that's not bad enough, circus owners keep their animals in tiny (iii) _____ and transport them all around the country in (iv) _____ barely big enough for them to fit into. And what about the equestrian world? The wild, natural (v) _____ of the horse is 'broken' out of it (that is even the verb horse-breakers use...) and it is 'trained' - again with a whip - to be obedient and forced to race or jump, and risk serious harm in the process. And what happens when a horse gets injured? The owners simply get it (vi) _____ . We even use animals to carry out laboratory (vii) _____ . We test new (viii) _____ and new drugs on animals, and we force them to endure all kinds of pain in the process. The zoo is supposed to be a safe (ix) _____ though, right? Wrong. In many poor countries, zoo animals are mistreated and left (x) _____ and lonely for lack of (xi) _____ . And as for pets, well, we simply objectify them and treat them likes toys if they're lucky. If not, we (xii) _____ them or (xiii) _____ them for the most part.

cures	extinct	companionship	cosmetics	cruelty	cages
humane	research	unstimulated	put down	conservation	pleasure
neglect	respect	haven	educate	appreciate	spirit
abandon	companions	tests	enclosures	endangered	

(C) This is a Part 2 question. Try to answer it using the *step-by-step* approach.

> Describe a time you went to a performance or visited an attraction that involved animals in some way.
>
> In your answer you should say:
> - when and where you went
> - why you went
> - what you saw
>
> and whether or not you enjoyed it.

Step ① Make Notes

_____

_____

_____

_____

_____

_____

_____

_____

_____

Step ② Write Answer

_____

_____

_____

_____

_____

_____

_____

_____

_____

Step ③ Speak

(D) Remember, in Part 2, the examiner may ask you some follow-up questions. Discuss these questions with a partner.

- Do you like the circus / the zoo? Why / why not?
- Do you like pets? Would you describe yourself as an animal person?
- Are you scared of any animals?

(E) Remember, Part 3 is always related to the topic in Part 2. Answer these Part 3 questions. First, write your answers down. Then put away your written answers and try to say the answers using similar ideas (but do not try to memorise your written answers).

1. 'People generally treat animals quite well.' Do you agree?

_____

_____

_____

_____

2. 'An animal life is not worth the same as that of a human.' Do you agree?

_____

_____

_____

_____

_____

3. Do you think it is necessary to test out products on animals?

_____

_____

_____

_____

_____

4. Is it cruel to keep animals in zoos or make them perform in the circus?

_____

_____

_____

_____

5. Is it right for people to keep exotic animals as pets?

_____

_____

_____

_____

(F) Look at the statements / phrases below and decide whether they relate to **(a) a pet dog**, **(b) a pet cat**, or **(c) a pet rabbit**. Be prepared to justify your decisions.

(1) very loyal

(2) very independent

(3) very affectionate

(4) Wanders off on its own a lot

(5) Loves attention

(6) cute, soft and furry

(7) NEEDS A LOT OF CARE – VERY RELIANT ON OWNER

(8) low-maintenance

(9) HIGHLY INTELLIGENT

(10) RESPONSIVE TO COMMANDS

(11) good at alerting to danger and keeping watch

(12) Need to clean up after it

(13) sheds a lot of hair

(14) Very delicate and easily hurt

(15) EASY TO TRAIN

(a) Dog:	(b) Cat:	(c) Rabbit:
Add your own:	Add your own:	Add your own:

(G) Look at the pictures and answer the questions below, discussing them with a partner or as a class.

- Which of these pets would you rather have?
- Which of these pets do you think would be the easiest to look after?
- Which of them do you think would be the most difficult to look after?
- Is there a type of pet that is not pictured here that you would like to own?
- What pets do you have at the moment?

(H) Answer the following Part 2 question using the *step-by-step* approach.

Describe your perfect pet.

In your answer you should say:

- what type of animal it would be
- what it would look like
- how it would behave

And why it would make such a good pet.

Follow-up Questions:
- Have you ever had a pet that gave you trouble?
- Do you think you would be (are) a good pet owner?
- What would you do if you found an abandoned pet by the side of the street?

IELTS Speaking

Step **1** *Notes*

_____
_____
_____
_____
_____
_____
_____
_____

Step **2** *Write Answer*

_____
_____
_____
_____
_____
_____
_____
_____
_____

Step **3** *Speak*

(H) Answer the following Part 3 questions on a related topic.

- Why do people become so attached to their pets?
- Do you think it is strange when people like being around pets more than human beings?
- Do you think it is cruel to race and jump horses?
- Are people who hunt animals for their own entertainment doing anything wrong?
- Why do most people not eat cats and dogs, yet they do eat cows and pigs?
  What's the difference?

Unit 4

Speaking Test 4

PART 1

The examiner will ask you some questions about yourself.

Let's talk about pets.
Do you have any pets?
Do you like animals?
What pet would you get if you could choose any?
How does the rest of your family feel about pets?
Have you ever had a bad experience with an animal?

The examiner will then ask you some questions about one or two other topics. See the example below.

Now let's talk about food.
What's your favourite food?
Do you eat out at restaurants often?
Do you eat a lot of fast food?
Do you like food from other countries?
What sorts of food do you and your friends eat when you go out together?

PART 2

The examiner will give you a topic on a card like the one below and ask you to talk about it for one to two minutes. Before you talk you have one minute to think about what you want to say. The examiner will give you some paper and a pencil so you can make notes if you want to.

> Describe your favourite animal.
>
> You should say:
>
> - what it is and what it looks like
> - where it is found
> - how it behaves
>
> and explain why you like it.

The examiner may ask you one or two more related questions when you have finished, like those given in the example below.

Do you ever watch nature documentaries on television?
Would you like to work with animals?
Would you ever think of becoming a vegetarian?

PART 3

The examiner will ask you some more general questions which follow on from the topic in Part 2.

Do you think being cruel to an animal is the same as being cruel to a human?
Should people be allowed to hunt animals for their own entertainment?
How can we help protect endangered species of animals?
What sorts of human activities make it more difficult for wild animals to survive?
Is it fair to make pets out of wild animals?
If a shark kills a human in the sea, should it be hunted down?
'There are no intelligent animals - except humans...' Do you agree?

Unit 5 Home

(A) Look at the pictures above and discuss these questions with a partner or as a class:

- Which of these homes would you least like to live in? Why?
- Which would be your preferred choice to live in? Why?
- Which is most similar to where you live at the moment?
- What are the good and bad things about living in the city?
- What are the good and bad things about living in the countryside?
- Is it better to live in the city or the countryside?

Useful Vocabulary

About where you live....

City/Town	large city ... medium-sized town ... small village ... in the suburbs ... in the city centre
Position	in the mountains ... on the coast ... by the sea ... by the river ... in the north of
Description	the capital of ... in a rural / industrial / commercial area ... has a population of ... is famous for
Area	convenient ... crowded ... noisy ... modern ... run-down ... traditional ... friendly ... isolated safe ... clean ... tidy ... congested ... polluted ... leafy ... popular
Home-type	block of flats ... apartment complex ... semi-detached house ... bungalow ... townhouse country house ... cottage ... estate ... three-storey ... renting ... sharing ... bedsit ... studio
Features	large rear garden ... patio ... bedroom balconies ... views out over the city ... en-suite bathrooms large extension ... conservatory ... pool ... open-plan

(B) Using the *Useful Vocabulary* section to help you, prepare your answer to the question below following the *step-by-step* approach.

> Describe the area where you live.
> You should say:
> - whether you live in a town/village etc. and where it is
> - what general facts you know about your town/village etc.
> - what the area is like
>   and mention something about the type of accommodation you live in.

Step 1 Make some notes

(Remember that you don't have to speak about the points on the prompt-card in the order they appear, but make sure to cover them all.)

Step 2 Write your answer out in full

(Remember that you will not be given time to do this in the exam but for now writing your answer out is a good way of adding further structure to your thoughts and ordering them in your mind, which will help you to speak more fluently. Do not memorise your written answer as this defeats the purpose of the exercise.)

Step 3 Speak

(Cover your written answer and use your notes to help you speak for about two minutes.)

(C) Now we are going to do some revision. Look at exercises (i) and (ii) below. For (i) you should write the phrases/statements from the box in the correct positions in the table. For (ii), complete the diagram using the statements/phrases from the box. An example is done for you in each case.

Revision (i)	Part 1	Part 2	Part 3
Time		3-4 minutes	
Description			
Register		informal/neutral	
Testing			

- 4-5 minutes
- informal
- ~~informal/neutral~~
- your ability to analyse and discuss ideas in detail
- your ability to organise ideas and speak fluently
- you must take part in a discussion of general and abstract ideas related to the previous part
- your ability to talk about your personal experiences and interests
- you must answer questions about everyday topics
- you must present a short talk based on a topic given to you
- 4-5 minutes
- neutral/formal
- ~~3-4 minutes~~

Revision (ii)

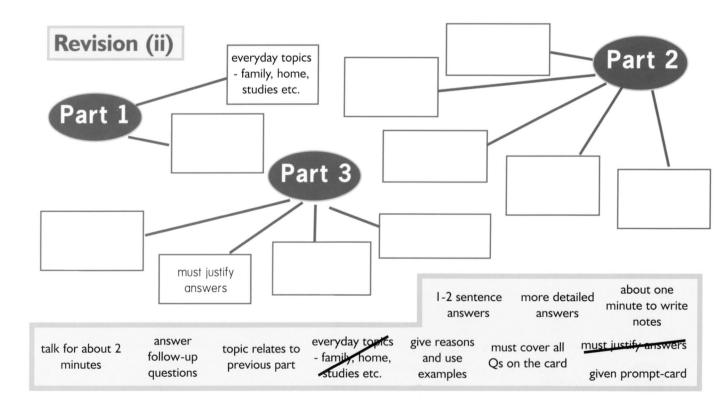

everyday topics - family, home, studies etc.

Part 1

Part 3

Part 2

must justify answers

1-2 sentence answers   more detailed answers   about one minute to write notes

talk for about 2 minutes   answer follow-up questions   topic relates to previous part   everyday topics - family, home, studies etc.   give reasons and use examples   must cover all Qs on the card   ~~must justify answers~~   given prompt-card

Speaking Test 5

Part 1

The examiner will ask you some questions about yourself.

Let's talk about your neighbourhood.

What is the area where you live like?

What is there to do there?

What is the house you live in like?

Who do you live with?

Would you prefer to live somewhere else?

The examiner will then ask you some questions about one or two other topics. See the example below.

Now let's talk about music.

What's your favourite type of music?

Do you play any musical instruments?

Do you have a favourite band?

Are you a good singer?

Do you like to perform in public?

Part 2

The examiner will give you a topic on a card like the one below and ask you to talk about it for one to two minutes. Before you talk you have one minute to think about what you want to say. The examiner will give you some paper and a pencil so you can make notes if you want to.

Describe your favourite place.
You should say:
- where it is located
- what it is like
- what there is to do there

and explain why you like it so much.

The examiner may ask you one or two more related questions when you have finished, like those given in the example below.

Do you think you will live where you are now for the rest of your life?

Where would you like to live if you could move home?

What kind of house would you like to own?

Part 3

The examiner will ask you some more general questions which follow on from the topic in Part 2.

Do you think it is better to own or rent your home?

Is owning a holiday home a good idea?

Should we let people build houses in the countryside?

What problems are caused by large numbers of people living together in cities?

What sorts of issues do people who live in remote areas have to deal with?

Why do some people want to live as far away from towns and cities as possible, do you think?

Unit 6 Education

(A) Read the text below and fill in the gaps with words from the box. Use each word only once.

holistic	funding	interactive
state	independent thinkers	practical
partnerships	applied	curriculum
discipline	rote-learning	
resources	teaching standards	

Beset by Problems

The education system is far from perfect and one of the main concerns in recent years has been how to maintain 1) _____ , with student behaviour, it seems, becoming ever more extreme and belligerent. Teachers have lost control of the classroom and little respect remains, which brings us to the next issue: 2) _____ . Granted teachers are not all to blame for the unruly behaviour of children in inner-city schools, and sure they need to be empowered to take the necessary steps to deal with behavioural problems, but it is likely that they would command more respect if their lessons were more effective and relevant - this is where training comes in. Teachers also need to be familiar with all the gismos and gadgets students seem so eager to embrace - all the more reason for the rapid introduction of technology into the classroom. Research has proven that the modern student responds more effectively when 3) _____ stimuli (whiteboards etc.) are employed. The broadening of the 4) _____ is also essential; it must include 5) _____ and 6) _____ courses, as well as academic ones. And there must be a move away from 7) _____ ; students must be encouraged to become 8) _____ . Nearly all 9) _____ schools lack sufficient 10) _____ and 11) _____ , and it seems unlikely the government will be able to provide extra funding, so surely a new approach must be considered - public-private 12) _____ - perhaps companies may be willing to provide the funding shortfall. But, above all, school must become a 13) _____ endeavour; education must be about more than just what goes on inside the classroom; it must encourage students' general development and look after their broader welfare.

(B) Answer the following questions related to the text either with a partner or as part of a class discussion.

(i) In your experience, is discipline a big problem in schools today? Give examples or reasons to back up your answer.

(ii) What about the standard of teaching - do you think the majority of teachers are good at their job or not?

(iii) Do you think students would respond better to lessons if more technology was introduced? Why / Why not?

(iv) How would you change the school curriculum if you had the opportunity to? What subjects would you add or remove?

(v) Should all young people be sent to school? Why / why not?

(vi) What do you think could be done generally to improve the education system?

(vii) How do you think the schools of the future will be different? Will there be online classrooms instead of actual classrooms? Will there be virtual teachers? Etc.

(C) Match the words/phrases on the left to the definitions on the right. You will not need to use all the options.

1. hike (in something)
2. fees
3. elite
4. marginalise
5. grant
6. grammar schools
7. league tables

(i)   leave someone or something isolated
(ii) rise
(iii) the best at anything
(iv) a way of graphing performance within a group
(v)   institutes of scholarly excellence
(vi) charges
(vii) a sum of money provided to a person or organisation, usually with no requirement for it to be repaid
(viii) a school which focuses on learning the structures of language
(ix) leave someone or something behind
(x)   a method of outlining information in note form

(D) Listen to the Recording and answer these questions in your own words based on the information that you hear.

(i) What is happening to higher education fees according to the speaker?

_____
_____
_____

(ii) Apart from scholarships and grants, what other option do poor students have to fund their higher education? What is the problem with this option?

_____
_____
_____

(iii) What effect does the speaker say the fees issue is having on society?

_____
_____
_____

(E) Compare your answers to (D) with a partner's and then talk about the following questions, either with them or as part of a class discussion. [These questions are similar in style to those found in Part 3 of the IELTS Speaking test.]

- Do you think rich people have an advantage over poorer people in terms of getting a good education?
- Is the society we live in a class-based one where there are different rules for rich people and poor people?
- Are paid-for private schools better than state schools? Why / why not?
- Why are some universities like Cambridge and Oxford better-respected than others?
  Do you think it is fair for these universities to charge higher fees?
- What could be done to make higher education more accessible for all types of students?
- Should higher education be free?
- Do you think the amount of money you have is a sign of how smart you are?

(F) Look at the pictures. They show teachers of all sorts. Do any of the teachers in the pictures remind you of ones you have had? Discuss the following questions with a partner:

- What qualities should a teacher have?
- What qualities are not desirable in a teacher?

Once you have discussed the questions together, write down as many qualities as you can think of to go in each box.

Good Qualities:	Bad Qualities:

(G) Listen to the Recording and find an example in what you hear to show that the teacher exhibited each characteristic (i-vi) below. Write the example beside the characteristic.(i) has been done for you.

(i)   cheerful   *always greeted the students with a big smile on his face* _____

(ii) interesting   _____

(iii) sensitive to the students' needs

        _____

(iv) passionate in a way that rubs off on students

        _____

(vi) fair   _____

NOTE: In the recording, when the speaker makes a point about the teacher's character, she gives an example to support her point. This is good practice to follow for you, too. Always use examples to support what you say.

(H) Listen to the recording and find an example in what you hear to show that the teacher exhibited each characteristic (i-iv) below. Write the example beside the characteristic. (i) has been done for you.

(i)   selfish   _always wanted to be the centre of attention and wanted students to notice her_

(ii) unprofessional _____

(iii) unprepared   _____

(iv) unfair   _____

(I) Match the characteristics in Table A with their opposites in Table B.

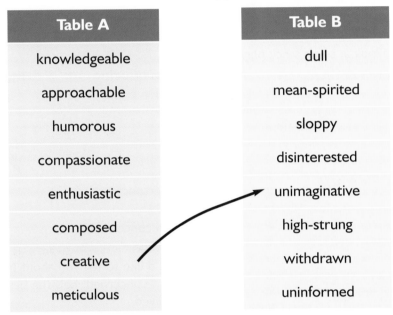

Table A	Table B
knowledgeable	dull
approachable	mean-spirited
humorous	sloppy
compassionate	disinterested
enthusiastic	unimaginative
composed	high-strung
creative	withdrawn
meticulous	uninformed

(J) Put the words from the box below in the right section - Good Teacher or Bad Teacher - as in the example.

GOOD TEACHER

_____

_____

_____

BAD TEACHER

picky

_____

_____

_____

level-headed	moody	alert	charismatic	strict	tolerant	condescending
edgy	monotonous	arrogant	dismissive	lenient	sincere	dependable
engaging	committed	absent-minded	demanding	picky	conceited	witty

71

IELTS Speaking

(K) This is an example of an IELTS Speaking Part 2 task. Read the question.

> Describe your favourite teacher.
> You should say:
> - who the person was
> - what kind of a person they were
> - what their lessons were like
> and explain why you liked them so much.

Before you give your talk, let's take a look at some stock phrases.

- 'I'd like to tell you about…'
- 'I've chosen to talk about…'
- 'The subject of my talk is…'
- 'I'm going to tell you about…'
- 'What I want to talk about is…'
- 'The person I am going to talk about is…'
- 'I've decided to talk about…'
- 'I'd like to tell you about…'

[the next three are more difficult]

- 'The moment I read the instructions, I knew what I was going to say; I'd like to tell you about…'

- 'I'm really pleased this topic came up because there are lots of things I want to say; I'm going to talk about…'

- 'Well, when I read the instructions, I immediately knew what I wanted to do; I am going to talk about…'

Introducing the topic

Moving the talk on

- 'You see, …'
- 'To me, …'
- 'From my perspective, …'
- 'For me, …'
- 'As far as I'm concerned, …'

Example: I'd like to tell you about Mr. Welsh. As far as I'm concerned, he's the best teacher that's ever lived.

Example: The person I'm going to talk about is Miss Daly. For me, Miss Daly is an inspiration.

Example: I'm really pleased this topic came up because there are lots of things I want to say; I'm going to talk about a teacher named Mr. Wallace. You see, Mr. Wallace was no ordinary teacher; he was one of a kind.

Remember:

Your account does not have to be accurate; this is not a test of memory but a test of English - the examiner is not going to know or really care whether you are making it up or telling a real story.

That said, it is always easier to talk about something if you have experienced and genuinely believe what you are saying, so try to choose a subject (in this case a person) that you do know, and have experience and a relevant opinion of.

But, whatever you do, don't complicate the talk for yourself just so that what you say is completely true.

If your favourite teacher Michel was an eccentric, half-Canadian, quarter-Korean, quarter-Irish, former National Hockey League star for the Canucks, third-cousin of the Queen of England, substitute that you had for two weeks and three days of the first term of first year of secondary school, who taught you again for one week and three days in the second term of third year, no one will hold it against you if you don't mention every last detail…

What you should always do, though, is GIVE EXAMPLES to justify what you say. If you say National-Hockey-League Michael was a kind teacher, then support this by mentioning the time when he saw you were having difficulty and how he sat down with you after class and went through the problem material slowly, step-by-step until you finally understood it.

Now, let's try to answer (K) using the step-by-step approach.

Step 1 **Make Notes**

_____

_____

_____

_____

_____

_____

_____

_____

Step 2 *Write Answer*

_____

_____

_____

_____

_____

_____

_____

_____

Step 3 *Speak*

(L) Look at the example answer below and choose the correct linking expression to fill each gap from the three choices given. The first one is done for you.

I think Religion is one of the hardest subjects of all to teach and make interesting. **(1)** _Despite_ this, my favourite teacher is Ms. Kim, my third-year Religion teacher. *[In spite / Despite / For]*

Ms. Kim was quite young - perhaps twenty-three - and she had no prior experience in the classroom. **(2)** _____ , you would never have guessed it as her teaching style was far more effective and she was far more confident than most of the more experienced teachers around her. *[Moreover / However / As a result]*

I guess I probably had a slight crush on Ms. Kim, too. **(3)** _____ , she was very very attractive and she always had a beaming wide smile on her face. *[After all / Therefore / Additionally]*

She was so nice in fact that, **(4)** _____ we were a class of mischievous boys, we never said anything bad about her, teased her, or were rude or naughty around her - we just couldn't do it; she was too kind. *[if / even though / apart from]*

I remember, on the first day, when she walked into the room, we were all thinking, 'this is going to be too easy' - a young, naive, pretty teacher we could all tease and make fun of. **(5)** _____ , one of the boys asked her a silly, embarrassing question to test her out, but she answered him in the most honest, sincere and understanding way we'd ever seen. *[In case / Nonetheless / Naturally]*

It was like even though she knew he was being naughty, she wasn't upset by it. **(6)** _____ , she just had a love of kids, and the kind of patience and empathy needed to work with them. *[Clearly / In spite of this / Consequently]*

After that we never said anything bad to her again. **(7)** _____ , we sort of became her bodyguards - her defenders! *[In fact / After all / At last]*

You see, Ms. Kim was a good person and she showed us understanding where most of the other teachers would just criticize. **8)** _____ , for that, I guess we kind of 'loved' her, too. *[As / So / Yet]*

She was an inspiration **(9)** _____ ; her lessons were always so interesting and relevant - always about something we, as young people, could relate to. *[eventually / really / therefore]*

(10) _____ , she never, for one single lesson, used a book; she always did up her own notes and followed her own plans - I have never seen anything like it before or since. *[What's more / Nevertheless / Therefore]*

She was utterly dedicated and totally focused on getting us to interact with her. **(11)** _____ , in every single lesson, she would have 'student speak' time, where we would all get to have our say - to talk about something important to us. *[For example / Such as / Nonetheless]*

And everyone felt comfortable - from the shy students to the more outspoken ones. There was only one rule in Ms. Kim's class - respect. **(12)** _____ you respected the other students, you were a valued member of the class. *[So long as / As far as / Until]*

(13) _____ , if you didn't, Ms. Kim would not tolerate it. No bullying; everyone was equal and everyone's opinion mattered equally. *[Therefore / Consequently / That said]*

(14) _____ why I liked Ms. Kim so much, I think it must be obvious. She led by example and she commanded our respect. *[For / As for / As a consequence]*

She was totally committed to her job and she was totally devoted to her students. **(15)** _____ , she was just about the nicest person I think has ever lived! *[Aside / Besides / Instead]*

Speaking Test 6

Part I

The examiner will ask you some questions about yourself.

Let's talk about your schooling.

Where did you go to primary school?

Did/do you enjoy school?

What was/is your favourite school subject?

What was/is your least favourite school subject?

What did you study/do you want to study/are you studying at university?

The examiner will then ask you some questions about one or two other topics. See the example below.

Now let's talk about keeping fit.

Do you try to keep fit? How?

Do you think it is important for young people to stay fit?

Do you play any sports? Which do you like best?

Do you prefer team or individual sports?

Do you prefer watching sport or taking part?

Have you ever been to a live sports event?

Part 2

The examiner will give you a topic on a card like the one below and ask you to talk about it for one to two minutes. Before you talk you have one minute to think about what you want to say. The examiner will give you some paper and a pencil so you can make notes if you want to.

> Describe a teacher who you really did not like.
>
> You should say:
>
> - who the teacher was
> - what kind of person they were
> - what their lessons were like
>
> and explain why you didn't like them.

The examiner may ask you one or two more related questions when you have finished, like those given in the example below.

Do you think anyone can be a good teacher with practice?

What qualities do you think a good teacher should have?

Would you like to be a teacher? Why / why not?

Part 3

The examiner will ask you some more general questions which follow on from the topic in Part 2.

Do you think the majority of teachers are good at their job?

Teachers often complain about being overworked. Do you agree?

What can be done to improve the quality of teaching in schools?

Should teachers be allowed to hit students who misbehave very badly?

What do you think can be done to improve discipline in schools?

What would you do to improve the education system if you were the Minister for Education?

(A) Look at the pictures above. They show different kinds of natural disasters.
How many can you think of? Write the names of as many different types of natural disasters as you can think of in space provided below.

Avalanche
_____
_____
_____

(B) Compare your list with a partner's. Then, talk about these questions with them, or as part of a class discussion.

- What types of natural disasters are the most serious and deadly?
- What types of natural disasters are the most common?
- What types of natural disasters are the most rare?
- What types of natural disasters are of most concern where you live?
- What consequences can a serious natural disaster have?
- Have you ever experienced a natural disaster yourself?
- What well-known recent natural disasters can you think of?
- How do you think you would feel if you were caught up in a natural disaster?
- What would you do if there were an earthquake right now?
- What do you think of 'danger lovers' and 'thrill seekers' who go chasing after storms?

(C) Create a list of your top five most serious and deadly types of natural disasters.

(i) _____   (iv) _____

(ii) _____   (v) _____

(iii) _____

Compare these with your partner's list and try to justify your choices.

(D) Listen to the Recording and put the notes in the box in the right order (the exact order in which they are heard).

Dealing with the Threat of a Tsunami

Check your risk level:

Examine your location - is it a low-lying area...

_____

_____

Prepare:

_____

_____

_____

Be Alert:

_____

_____

_____

If Tsunami is about to strike:

_____

_____

_____

(i) Climb a tree

(ii) Listen out for warning sirens

(iii) Develop an escape plan

(iv) Check for signs erected in the area warning of the threat

(v) Head to the top of a well-built structure

(vi) Examine your location - is it a low-lying area near the coast?

(vii) Get an emergency pack ready

(viii) Look into your area's history

(ix) Be very aware of heightened threat-level after an earthquake

(x) Head away from coast to high ground

(xi) Watch out for sudden sea-level changes

(E) Listen to the recording and put the notes in the box in the right order (the exact order in which they are heard).

Preparing for a Hurricane

Shelter

- Choose a windowless room

_____

Supplies

_____

_____

_____

_____

Home and Garden

_____

_____

_____

_____

(i) Or take it into the house with you

(ii) Enough to last at least two weeks

(iii) Choose a windowless room

(iv) Board up all windows and glass doors

(v) Get together your flashlights, first-aid kit, clothing and battery supplies

(vi) Must be on the bottom floor of house

(vii) Buy canned food

(viii) Build a sturdy outdoor shelter for your pet

(ix) Purchase bottled water

(x) Put loose objects left outside away properly

(F) Now, with a partner, decide who Person A is and who Person B is. Person A will use the notes to tell Person B how to deal with a Tsunami threat and Person B will tell Person A how to prepare for a hurricane.

(G) Look at the pictures. They show problems for the environment and nature that are caused by human activity. Match the problem (Table A) with the damage it causes (Table B).

Table A	Table B
oil slick / oil spill	huge areas of land are carpet-bombed
global warming	endangered species of animals are hunted and killed illegally
deforestation	acid rain forms in the atmosphere
smog and pollution	fish suffocate and birds cannot fly
poaching	radiation exposure kills some and other animals are born deformed
war	ice in the polar regions melts leading to higher sea levels
nuclear fallout	the soil becomes weak and dry and turns to dust

(H) Can you think of any more problems caused by global warming? Write as many as you can in the box below.

- more severe storms and extreme weather

Compare your list with your partner's, then talk about the questions below, either with them or as part of a class discussion.

(i) What are the main causes of global warming?

(ii) What can we do to find a solution to the problem?

(iii) Why do some people buy clothes and ornaments made from the skin or body parts of endangered species? What should be done about this issue?

(iv) Nothing, not even nature, can get in the way of progress - do you agree?

(v) Do you think Planet Earth has a future?

(vi) Can you think of any endangered species? What are the reasons they are so rare?

(I) First, decide with your partner which one of you is Person A and which is Person B. Person A should read the text labelled Text A. Person B should read the text labelled Text B

The Amur Leopard (Text A)

Leopards are rarely found in colder, high-elevation environments. Most of them live in the African savannah, where their numbers are fairly plentiful and stable. But the Amur is different. It lives in the temperate forests of the Russian Far East, and has to endure one of the harshest winters on the planet.

Its summer pelt is 1 inch thick, but, on account of the severe winter, its winter fur has to be 2 inches thicker. The fur itself is covered with widely-spaced circles. Amurs have longer legs than other leopard species; these legs are for walking in the snow. They also enable them to make powerful leaps when hunting - over 19 feet horizontally and about 9 feet vertically.

There are thought to be only about 30 individuals left in the wild today. This is down to a number of factors, all of which are related to human activity.

(i) Unsustainable logging: Foresters are cutting down trees at a faster rate than they can regrow, leaving the Amur without its natural habitat.
(ii) Forest fires: Most of these are caused by careless campers. Fire destroys vast areas of Amur habitat each year.
(iii) Land conversion: The demand for more farmland has meant that farmers have been taming more and more of the wilderness and using it for grazing.
(iv) Poaching: Amurs are highly-prized for their unique spotted fur.

Unless something is done to protect the few remaining wild Amurs, the species will become extinct.

The Iberian Lynx (Text B)

The Iberian Lynx was once very common throughout much of Southern France and the Iberian Peninsula (Spain and Portugal). As recently as 1990, there were thought to be 1,100 individuals in the wild. But that number has now reduced dramatically and a 1998 study found there to be fewer than 200 left in existence.

Iberians live in a mixture of different habitats, but prefer a combination of dense scrubland or forest for shelter and open pasture for hunting. Rabbits account for about 80% of the Iberian's diet, with the remainder made up of rodent, hare, juvenile and fallow deer, and wild bird kills. The Iberian has excellent senses of smell and sight which make it a very able hunter. Other than when mating, it tends to be a very solitary creature and always hunts alone.

Its main challenge today is starvation due to lack of food. Epidemics of diseases like myxomatosis wiped out much of the rabbit population over the last 50 years and left the Iberian in a very vulnerable position, given its reliance on this type of prey. Habitat loss has also been a major factor in the dramatic fall in Iberian population numbers - some 80% of its range has been lost to farmland, buildings and other infrastructure. Road accidents are also very common and account for a large number of deaths each year.

The Iberian is now classified as a critically endangered species and efforts are under way to help it recover. These mainly entail creating and conserving habitat in which the cat is likely to prosper and trying to grow the rabbit population.

Read over your text (A or B) a second time and then allow yourself about one minute to make some notes on it. Only allow yourself a minute and make your notes very short.

Notes on the Amur Leopard
Habitat - not so usual:

_____

_____

Characteristics and Features

_____

_____

Current Population and Threats

_____

_____

_____

_____

Notes on the Iberian Lynx
Population - Past and present:

_____

_____

Habitat and Prey:

_____

_____

Challenges Faced by the Iberian Lynx

_____

_____

Efforts to help it:

_____

_____

IELTS Speaking

(J) Now, Person A, using only your notes, tell Person B about the Amur Leopard's situation. Person B, fill in the notes on the Amur Leopard based on what you hear.

(K) Now, Person B, using only your notes, tell Person A about the Iberian Lynx's situation. Person A, fill in the notes on the Iberian Lynx based on what you hear.

Once this is done, Person A should report on the Iberian Lynx to the class and Person B should report on the situation of the Amur Leopard.

> **NOTE:**
>
> The focus until now in the units has generally been on getting used to note-taking and speaking with notes. There has been no emphasis on time. Well, in exercise (H) you were given a time limit, and, from now on, there will be a time limit for each task where you are asked to take notes. This will give you practice at identifying and noting down the few key points of the subject as quickly as possible under time constraints - a skill which is essential to Part 2 of the Speaking.

(L) Let's take a look at this Part 2 question.

> Describe a time when you experienced very bad weather
>
> You should say:
> - where you were and who you were with
> - what the weather was like
> - what you did in the situation
>
> and explain how you felt during the experience.

(i) You will now hear a Recording in which this question is answered. Listen carefully and note down the key points - only worry about the key points; don't try to write down lots of things. 🎧

Notes on 'the Big Snow'

Where and who with:

_____

_____

What the weather was like:

_____

_____

_____

What the speaker did:

_____

_____

_____

_____

How the speaker felt:

_____

_____

_____

(ii) Compare your notes with your partner's. Then take it in turns and tell the story yourselves. Tell the story as though you were the person it happened to. Use your notes to help you.

M) Now try to answer the question in **(K)** yourself using the step-by-step approach, but this time only allow yourself **one minute** to make notes.

Step (1) **Make Notes**

_____

_____

_____

_____

_____

_____

_____

_____

Step (2) **Write Answer**

_____

_____

_____

_____

_____

_____

_____

_____

Step (3) **Speak**

(N) Look at the pictures above. They show different ways we can help the environment.
What can you as an individual do to help protect the environment? Write as many things as you can think of down in the box.

Turn off lights not in use

_____

Compare your ideas with your partner's. Then answer the following questions, either with your partner or as part of a class discussion.

- Do you recycle? What kinds of things do you recycle?
- Apart from recycling, what can each of us do to help protect the environment?
- Do you ever litter?
- Is there a big litter problem in your area?
- Is pollution a big problem where you live?
- Are you concerned about protecting the environment?
- Is it really possible for one person to make a difference in terms of helping protect the environment?
- Why should we try to protect the environment - why is it important?

Unit 7

(O) Divide the following into things we can do as individuals to help protect the environment, and things only society as a whole (or the government) can do.

(i) use renewable sources of energy to supply homes and businesses

(ii) replant areas of forest that have been cut down

(iii) car pool when we go to work

(iv) cut down on the number of plane journeys we take each year.

(v) give people tax incentives to buy electric cars

(vi) tax factories based on how much they pollute

(vii) put all our food waste in the compost

(viii) give people grants to put up solar panels and better insulate their homes

(ix) plant trees and shrubs in our gardens

(x) volunteer to help out with clean-up projects in the neighbourhood

(xi) only use hot water when we really need to such as for washing ourselves

(xii) only put on the washing machine or dishwasher when there is a full load

(xiii) make it easier to recycle by providing more recycling depots

(xiv) penalize households that do not separate their waste into recyclable and non-recyclable goods

(xv) improve the public transport system so as to encourage more people to use it

(xvi) collect rainwater for watering plants

Society / Government	Individuals
(i) use renewable sources of energy to supply homes and businesses	

Add some more ideas of your own for what society as a whole and the government can do.

Compare your answers and ideas with your partner's. Then ask each other the following questions:

(i) What steps can the government take to help protect the environment?

(ii) Should the government issue penalties to people and businesses which pollute and damage the environment? If yes, what kinds of penalties do you suggest?

(iii) What types of businesses are the biggest environmental polluters, do you think?

IELTS Speaking

(P) Look at the Part 2 question below.

> Describe something you do regularly that helps protect the environment
> You should say:
> - what it is
> - how often you do it
> - what it involves
> and explain how it helps protect the environment.

(i) You will now hear a Recording in which this question is answered. Listen carefully and note down the key points - only worry about the key points; don't try to write down lots of things.

Notes on 'Something I do to Help Protect the Environment'

What it is: _____

How often you do it: _____

What it involves: _____
_____
_____
_____

How it helps protect the environment: _____
_____
_____

(ii) Compare your notes with your partner's. Then take it in turns and tell the story yourself. Tell the story as though you were the person saying it in the recording. Use your notes to help you.

(iii) Now try to answer these follow-up questions with your partner. [Remember, in Part 2, after your talk, you will also be expected to discuss some related questions].
- Are you happy with the amount you recycle?
- In what other ways do you think you could help protect the environment?
- Do you really care about protecting the environment? Why / why not?

- Then take it in turns to ask each other the following Part 3 questions:
- What kinds of human activities have damaged the environment?
- What consequences does the damage we have done to the environment have for wild animals?
- Are we more aware of environmental issues than we used to be?
- What is the biggest environmental problem we are faced with today?
- Is there a way to encourage companies to become more environmentally friendly?

(Q) Now try to answer the main question in (O) yourself using the step-by-step approach, but this time only allow yourself one minute to make notes.

Step ① Make Notes

_____
_____
_____
_____
_____

Step 2   *Write Answer*

_____

_____

_____

_____

_____

_____

_____

Step 3   *Speak*

Speaking Test 7

Part 1

The examiner will ask you some questions about yourself.

Let's talk about the environment around where you live.
What do you do to help protect your local environment?
How often do you recycle?

Is pollution a problem in your area?
What kinds of things do you recycle?
Do you ever throw rubbish on the ground?

The examiner will then ask you some questions about one or two other topics. See the example below.

Now let's talk about Art and Culture.
Are you any good at painting or making things with your hands?
Are there any national celebrations in your country?
Do you know of any celebrations from other cultures?

Do you like to visit museums and art galleries?
Would you like to be an artist?
What is your favourite celebration?

Part 2

The examiner will give you a topic on a card like the one below and ask you to talk about it for one to two minutes. Before you talk you have one minute to think about what you want to say. The examiner will give you some paper and a pencil so you can make notes if you want to.

> Describe a time you saw a rare or endangered animal
>   You should say:
>   • what type of animal you saw
>   • where you saw the animal
>   • what the animal looked like and how it behaved
> and explain how seeing this animal made you feel.

The examiner may ask you one or two more related questions when you have finished, like those given in the example below.

Have you ever volunteered to help protect wild animals or do something for the environment? (Would you like to?)
What very endangered species of animals can you think of? (Do you know why they are endangered?)
Would you like to work with wild animals?
Would you like to be a conservationist (someone whose job involves trying to protect the environment)?

Part 3

The examiner will ask you some more general questions which follow on from the topic in Part 2.
How do human activities cause problems for wild animals?
Why do some humans continue to illegally hunt rare and endangered wild animals?
What problems can global warming cause for wild animals?
Are humans to blame for global warming?
Do people today care about protecting the environment or are they not really worried?
What measures can governments take to try to reduce the effects of global warming and help protect the environment?

Unit 8 Technology

(A) Look at the pictures above. They show different kinds of modern technology.
What kinds of modern technology do you and your friends use? Write the names of as many different types as you can think of in the box below.

> Smartphone

(B) Compare your list with your partner's. Then, talk about these questions with them, or as part of a class discussion.

- What is the most useful piece of technology you own?
- What piece of modern technology would you say you use most often?
- What do you think is the best new technology ever invented?
- What are the benefits of the Internet?
- What do you use your mobile phone for?
- Are there any drawbacks to new technology? If so, what are they?

(C) Make a list of the top ten technological inventions.

1. _____
2. _____
3. _____
4. _____
5. _____

6. _____
7. _____
8. _____
9. _____
10. _____

Compare these with your partner's list and try to justify your choices. Agree on the two best inventions of all and report back to the class.

(D) (i) Select one advantage and one disadvantage from the list below to write beside each technological invention. An example has been done for you. Choose the best fit where more than one is possible.

The Smartphone

Advantage

_____

_____

Disadvantage
Much shorter battery life than older models

_____

The Internet

Advantage

_____

_____

Disadvantage

_____

_____

Facebook

Advantage

_____

_____

Disadvantage

_____

_____

E-shopping Websites

Advantage

_____

_____

Disadvantage

_____

_____

Laptop

Advantage

_____

_____

Disadvantage

_____

_____

(i)	Counts as extra hand luggage if you carry it separately when you go on holiday	**(vi)**	Very small multi-function portable device
(ii)	Can order from the comfort of your own home	**(vii)**	Still a lot of cyber attacks and your personal information may be stolen
(iii)	Encourages people to interact online rather than face-to-face	**(viii)**	Can keep track of what friends are doing all the time
(iv)	Allows you to download and stream films	**(ix)**	Cannot 'try before you buy'
(v)	Much shorter battery life than older models	**(x)**	A light, easy-to-carry, fully functional workstation

(ii) Now think of another advantage and disadvantage of each technological invention. Write the advantage or disadvantage on the second line underneath the answer you chose from the box.

(E) (i) Now, let's take a look at another piece of technology - the MP3 player. First of all, write down four good things about it. The first one is done for you.

1:     *very small and easy to carry* _____

2:     _____

3:     _____

4:     _____

(ii) Okay, so the MP3 player is very small and easy to carry ... so what? Explain why this is good... Say why each point you made in (i) is good.

1: *you can take it anywhere with you* _____

2: _____

3: _____

4: _____

(iii) Okay, so you can take an **MP3 player** anywhere with you ... like where? Give an example...

1: *to the gym* _____

2: _____

3: _____

4: _____

Now, if you look at what we've just done, we've (i) made a statement, then (ii) explained our statement, and finally (iii) given an example. This is basically the formula every time you answer a question that asks you for your opinion.

When giving an opinion   you should...

1 Make a statement

2 Explain the statement

3 Give an example / support the statement

(iv) Now let's link it all together...

To introduce your points use an 'ordering' linking word.

1st Point	First of all / First and foremost / To begin with / Firstly
2nd Point	Secondly / Furthermore / Second of all / And another thing / What's more
3rd Point	Thirdly / Furthermore / What's more / And another thing
Final Point	Lastly / Last of all / And last but not least / Finally

To explain your points use one of these phrases:
(i) This is good (or bad) because...
(ii) That's a big plus (or negative) as...
(iii) You see, that's good (or bad) because...
(iv) And that's a good (or bad) thing because...
(v) ...which is good (or bad) because...

To give an example, use one of these phrases:
(i) For instance, ...
(ii) For example, ...

Q: Why is an MP3 player a useful piece of technology?

Write your answer out in full below using the linking words to join your points together.

To begin with, an MP3 player is very small and easy to carry. That's a big plus as you can take it anywhere with you. For example, you can even carry it on you while you are exercising in the gym.

_____
_____
_____
_____
_____
_____
_____
_____
_____
_____
_____

(F) Now let's look at a Part 2 question.

> Describe a piece of technology you use a lot
>
> You should say:
>
> - what the piece of technology is
> - how often you use it
> - what you use it for
>
> and explain why it is so useful.

Answer the question using the step-by-step approach. But now, you have practised a lot, so it's time to remove Step 2. In the exam you don't have time for this. You have a minute or so to make notes and then you must speak. Allow yourself about a minute to make your notes, then answer the question verbally.

Step 1   Make Notes

_____

_____

_____

_____

_____

_____

_____

_____

_____

_____

Step 2   ~~Write Answer~~

Step 3   Speak

(G) Read the following short passage about laptop computers and fill in the gaps with suitable linking expressions from the box below. The first is done for you.

The Laptop Computer

Laptop computers used to be the favourite 'toy' of business people on the go when they first came out. Now they are so affordable that everyone has one these days. They have become less a luxury and more a necessity. Which begs the question; why?

Well, for a start, they are portable, which means we can take them with us wherever we go. **(1)** <u>_As well as_</u> this, of course, they are extremely practical; they give us access to potentially thousands of important work and personal documents at the press of a few buttons. **(2)** _____ to this, with the internet becoming such an important part of our lives, having online access no matter where you go has become essential - that's where the laptop comes in.

(3) _____ can you take it with you on business trips, but you can **(4)** _____ bring it away with you on holidays. This gives you the ability to check your emails, **(5)** _____ your social network and chat sites, **(6)** _____ .

(7) _____, technology has come so far today that it even allows you to have video calls with friends and colleagues using your laptop's webcam and in-built microphone. **(8)** _____ from that, your laptop is also a portable entertainment system these days, too. **(9)** _____ being able to play music, it also allows you to stream online films and watch DVDs. **(10)** _____, if you have a USB connector for your phone, you can also use it as a phone charger on the go. In truth, if you have a laptop with you, you have the world at your fingertips as well.

In addition	As well as	Furthermore	Too	Not to mention
As well as	In addition	Apart	Also	Not only

These are examples of 'listing' or 'supporting' linking expressions. They are generally used to link lists of things, ideas or points together.

Listing / Supporting Linking Expressions

<u>Separate point to previous sentence.</u>	<u>Two points in the same sentence</u>
Also / As well as that / And another thing , ...	Not only can ... , but ... also...
Furthermore, ...	Not only ... also...
What's more, ...	Apart from ... also...
Moreover, ...	... , not to mention ...
In addition (to this), ...	In addition to ... also...
Additionally, ...	As well as ... also...
..., too / also / as well.	... and ... , too / as well / also

Examples (two points in the same sentence):

- <u>Not only</u> can you use your smartphone to text people, <u>but</u> you can <u>also</u> use it to send emails.
- <u>Not only</u> is the internet free in many places, you can <u>also</u> log on almost anywhere.
- <u>Apart from</u> listening to music on MP4 players, you can <u>also</u> watch movies on them.
- You can play games on smart televisions, <u>not to mention</u> surf the internet.
- <u>In addition to</u> being very light and slim, tablet PCs are <u>also</u> very attractive looking style-wise.
- <u>As well as</u> being a lot more affordable today than ever before, modern laptop PCs <u>also</u> have more storage.
- Smartphones are practical <u>and</u> they are easy to use, <u>too</u>.

(H) (i) List at least six examples of the usefulness of the internet. Do not write full sentences, just use simple points. One is done for you already.

The Internet

1:	*can shop online*	5:	
2:		6:	
3:		7:	
4:		8:	

(ii) Now, turn your points into a well-linked set of simple sentences using some of the linking expressions we have just looked at. Only use the separate-point-to-previous-sentence expressions for now.

One of the main benefits of the internet is that you can shop online. As well as that, you can...

_____

_____

(I) Look at the following Part 2 question.

> Describe the most useful piece of technology you own.
>   You should say:
>   ● what the piece of technology is
>   ● what it looks like
>   ● how often you use it
> and list the different things you use it for.

Answer the question using the step-by-step approach. But now that you have practised a lot, it's time to remove Step 2. In the exam you don't have time for this. You have a minute or so to make notes and then you must speak. Allow yourself about a minute to make your notes, then answer the question verbally.

Step ① Make Notes

_____

_____

_____

_____

Step ~~② Write Answer~~   Step ③ Speak

(J) Talk about the following related Part 3 questions with a partner or as part of a class discussion.

- In what ways has the mobile phone made our lives easier?
- Are there any ways in which it has made our lives harder?
- What is the most important technological discovery of our time?
- What one piece of technology do you think we would struggle most to live without?
- How have technological advances affected the way we live?
- Has new technology made our lives better or worse overall?
- What new technologies would we be better off without?
- How has technology affected the way we interact with our friends and colleagues?
- What are the dangers associated with popular social networking sites?
- What sorts of dangers are associated with the internet?
- Is it safe to buy things over the internet?
- What does the future hold for us and how will our lives be different in 10 to 20 years from now?

(K) The pictures above show different things that might happen in the future, some more likely than others.

(i) Put the items below into one of the four columns of the table in accordance with how likely you think they are to happen within the next 25 years.

Almost Certain	Probable	Improbable	Almost certainly not

Within the next 25 years...

- ...we will go back to the moon.
- ...we will discover aliens.
- ...we will find a cure for cancer.
- ...we will find a cure for AIDS.
- ...we will discover the secret to everlasting life.
- ...we will land on the planet Mars.
- ...our planet will be destroyed.
- ...we will invent a way to travel long distances in an instant.
- ...we will all be part of one global nation.
- ...we will all speak the same language.
- ...we will create robots capable of doing all our work for us.
- ...we will build robots capable of feeling emotions.
- . ...we will be driving flying cars.
- . ...we will be going on holiday in space.
- ...we will be living on other planets
- ...we will live longer than we do today.

- . ...we will have a war that will result in billions of deaths.
- ...lots of our big cities will be underwater.
- ...many endangered species of animals will be extinct.
- ...most people will be obese and unhealthy.
- . ...we will be able to take pills to make ourselves smarter.
- ...we will be able to cure most serious diseases without hospital treatment.
- ...we will be able to predict the future.
- ...we will be able to control the weather.
- ...there will be no ice in the polar regions.
- ...the world will be much hotter.
- ...there will be another ice age.
- ...there will be no more war or crime.
- ...poverty will be eliminated.
- ...there will be a shortage of food and water.
- ...China will be the world's strongest and richest nation and Chinese will be the world's number one language.

(ii) Compare your answers with your partner's and try to justify your decisions where the two of you disagree. *Then open the topic up to a class discussion.*

Here are some stock phrases you can use when you want to talk about how probable something is. If you use the word in brackets, it is for emphasis; in other words, it is used to suggest something is even more or less probable.

Probable	Improbable
It is (highly) likely that....	I (highly) doubt that...
It seems (quite/very) probable that...	It's (highly) doubtful whether...
I would (really) expect that...	I can't (really) imagine that...
It seems (quite/very) likely (to me) that...	I think it is (highly) unlikely that...
I would imagine that...	It's (extremely) unlikely that...
In all likelihood, ...	It's (highly) improbable that...
In all probability...	It seems (extremely) unlikely that...
I'm quite sure that...	
I'm fairly certain that...	

(L) Look at the following Part 3 example question:

> *Do you think it is likely that people will live longer in the future?*

1 Make a statement

If you ask me, it is highly likely that people will live longer in the future.

2 Explain the statement

I would say that the average person will live between 5 and 10 years longer than they do today by about 2025.

3 Give an example / support the statement

My reasons for saying this are quite simple. First of all, **life expectancy has risen** steadily over the last 100 years or so. Secondly, **thanks to technological and medical advances**, more and more cures are being found for once deadly diseases. And even when a disease can't be cured, **the patient can expect to live longer** today than ever before. Thirdly, **we take better care of ourselves today than in the past**; we wash properly, we eat properly and our lives are much safer. <u>In short</u>, I think science and medicine will continue to advance quickly, and I think our living conditions and the way we look after ourselves will continue to improve. For these reasons, I have no doubt that we will live longer as time goes on.

When you want to conclude or summarise what you have said, there are a number of linking expressions you can use:

(i) In short   (ii) To sum up
(iii) In summary   (iv) In conclusion
(v) To conclude   (vi) To summarise

When you are talking about the future, it is unlikely that you will be able to give examples - after all, the future hasn't happened yet... - but you can give evidence to support your opinion, such as the information highlighted in bold here.

(i) Answer the following question in the same way. For now, write your answer first.

Do you think technology will be a lot more advanced in 10 or 15 years' time?

1 **Make a statement**

_____

2 **Explain the statement**

_____

_____

3 **Give an example / support the statement**

_____

_____

_____

_____

(ii) Answer the following question in the same way.

Do you think tourists will soon be regularly travelling into space on holiday?

1 **Make a statement**

_____

_____

2 **Explain the statement**

_____

_____

3 **Give an example / support the statement**

_____

_____

_____

_____

(iii) Now discuss your answers with your partner and ask each other the following additional questions, too:

How might everyday life be different for people 25 years from now?

Will there be more or fewer people living in the world in 25 years?

What would be the consequences for the world if, tomorrow, all the computers suddenly failed at the same time?

If you were able to travel through time to 100 years from now, what do you think you would see?

Is the future a bright one or should we be pessimistic about it?

Speaking Test 8

Part 1

The examiner will ask you some questions about yourself.

Let's talk about Computers.

Do you have your own computer at home? What do you use it for?

How often do you use a/your computer?

Do you have a separate games console? What sort of games do you play?

Are you good with technology?

What is your favourite piece of technology? What do you use it for?

The examiner will then ask you some questions about one or two other topics. See the example below.

Now let's talk about Your Friends

What does your best friend look like?

How long have you known them?

How does your best friend behave?

Would you confide in a friend if you had a problem?

Do you and your friends share the same interests?

What do you and your friends do together?

Part 2

The examiner will give you a topic on a card like the one below and ask you to talk about it for one to two minutes. Before you talk you have one minute to think about what you want to say. The examiner will give you some paper and a pencil so you can make notes if you want to.

> Describe the most expensive piece of technology you own
> You should say:
> - what the piece of technology is
> - how much it cost and where you bought it
> - what you use it for and how often you use it
> and whether or not you think it was good value for money.

The examiner may ask you one or two more related questions when you have finished, like those given in the example below.

Would you describe yourself as a 'tech person' - someone who is very interested in technology?

If you could buy any technological gadget, what would it be?

Do you think CD players are old-fashioned?

Do your parents know much about computers, smartphones and so on?

Part 3

The examiner will ask you some more general questions which follow on from the topic in Part 2.

Why do people often want to be one of the first to buy the latest gadgets?

Would a world without mobile phones be a better or worse place?

To what extent have computers become an important part of our lives?

What sorts of technological advances do you think we might see in the next 100 years?

Could we survive without modern technology, the way our great-grandparents, for example, did?

How has modern technology improved our lives?

How has it made our lives worse?

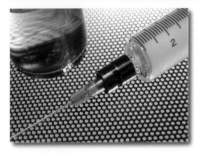

(A) Look at these pictures. They show different problems people have that might encourage them to turn to a life of crime. What do you think are the main causes of crime?

(i) Discuss this question with your partner and come up with as many causes as you can. Write them in the box.

> Greed (the desire to have lots more money than you need)

(B) Now that you have written down some causes of crime, come up with a top-five list, with (1) being the main cause of crime, (2) being the next-biggest cause etc. Do this on your own first.

(1) _____   (2) _____ (3) _____

(4) _____   (5) _____

Now compare this list with your partner's and agree on the two biggest causes of crime. *Open the topic up to a class discussion.*

(C) Talk about the following questions with your partner, or as part of a class discussion.

- Are all criminals bad?
- Are rich people less likely to be criminals than poor people?
- Do you think it is possible to turn over a new leaf? In other words, can a former criminal ever be trusted and become a valued member of society?
- Do you think you are capable of committing a crime in certain situations? If so, what situations?
- Are drink and drugs major factors in crime?
- What are the main causes of crime in your view?

(D) There are lots of different types of crime. How many can you think of?

Compare your list with your partner's and share any ideas either of you missed. Then discuss the following question together and agree on an answer.

What is the most serious type of crime?

When you want to agree or disagree with an opinion or idea, here are some useful phrases you can use.

Agree	Strongly Agree	Disagree	Strongly disagree
With a person: I see what you are saying... I see where you are coming from... What you say is true... I agree with you... We're in agreement... I feel the same way... I think so, too... With an idea I agree with the idea that... I support the idea that... I'm in favour of... I'm behind the idea that... I applaud the idea that...	With a person I completely agree... I couldn't agree more... You're absolutely right... I'm totally behind you... We're in complete agreement... I couldn't have said it better myself... With an idea I'm totally for the idea that... I'm completely behind the idea that... I'm totally in favour of... I'm very much in favour of the idea that... I completely agree with the notion that...	With a person I see what you are saying, but... We don't quite see eye to eye... I see where you are coming from, but... I know what you mean, but... I disagree because... I can't say I feel exactly the same way... I'm inclined to disagree with you... With an idea I'm against the idea of... I'm not in favour of... I don't support the idea that... I'm not behind the idea that... I don't agree that...	With a person I couldn't disagree more with what you are saying... I completely disagree with you... I feel the exact opposite... We're poles apart in our views... With an idea I'm totally against the idea that... I'm absolutely not in favour of... I am not at all behind the idea that... I'm not at all in favour of...

(E) (i) Match the type of crime in Table A with the right definition in Table B.

Table A		Answers
I	Petty Crime	G
2	Assault	
3	Homicide	
4	Manslaughter	
5	Perjury	
6	Mugging	
7	Stalking	
8	Fraud	
9	Arson	
10	Kidnapping	
11	Money Laundering	
12	Hijacking	
13	Theft	

	Table B
A	another name for murder, when one person deliberately sets out to and kills another
B	a violent physical attack on someone
C	an attack on a person motivated by a desire to rob them of the belongings they are carrying at the time
D	the crime of stealing from another person or organization
E	seizing and taking control of a vehicle by force
F	trying to hide the source of money made illegally
G	a minor crime such as pick-pocketing or shoplifting
H	deceiving or tricking people or organizations to make money out of them
I	deliberately setting private property on fire
J	lying in a court of law
K	following someone around everywhere without their permission
L	the murder of someone who you did not deliberately set out to murder
M	to take a person hostage and keep them locked up against their will (usually in the hope of getting some money for their safe return)

(ii) Discuss these questions with your partner or as a class:

(1) Is manslaughter any different to homicide? Can you think of a reason why someone might commit manslaughter?

(2) Which of these crimes is the least serious?

(3) For which of these crimes do you think a person should go to jail?

(4) Is self-defence an excuse for killing somebody?

The Story of John Ward

John Ward had been known to the police in the Irish county of Mayo for many years. He had over 80 convictions to his name. A middle-aged local farmer who lived alone had seen Ward snooping around his property a lot over the course of a few months. There had also been a spate of robberies at local farms in that time, too. The farmer was scared that his property would be next. In fact, so frightened and agitated was he that he used to sit in his shed for hours every day holding a gun. He also slept with it by his side. Then, one night in October 2006, the farmer saw Ward outside his house, creeping around. He took up his gun and fired at Ward. Ward was hit in the hip and badly injured. The farmer then walked up to Ward at close range and shot him once more. Ward was killed. In his trial the farmer claimed he was terrified that this man Ward would do him harm, and that he would come back and kill him if he let him escape. The farmer was found guilty of manslaughter and spent 6 years in prison. Then, in a retrial, the jury quashed his conviction and he was set free.

Premeditated Murder

If murder is premeditated, it is planned in advance - homicide.

(F) Read the story of John Ward and then discuss these questions with your partner.

(i) What would you have done if you were a member of the jury?

(ii) Do you think the farmer acted in self-defence?

(iii) What mitigating circumstance were there in the farmer's case?

(iv) What would you have done in the farmer's situation?

(v) Do you think it is right that the farmer was set free?

Mitigating Circumstances

If there are mitigating circumstances, there is information about the crime that makes it more understandable or makes you look at the criminal more sympathetically.

There are two ways of looking at the murder of John Ward. **On the one hand**, the farmer deliberately killed him. **On the other**, the farmer was so scared and worked up having been harassed for so long that he feared for his life and may genuinely have thought he was acting in self-defence. **On the one hand ... On the other, ...** is an example of a linking expression used to compare and contrast. Here are some more:

(i) In spite of...
(ii) Despite...
(iii) Despite this, ...
(iv) While...
(v) However, ...
(vi) That said, ...
(vii) Nonetheless, ...
(viii) Nevertheless, ...
(ix) ..., but...
(x) Even though...
(xi) Although...
(xii) ..., though...

(G) Use an appropriate linking expression to complete each of the following sentences (there is more than one correct answer in each case):

(i) _____**While**_____ it is never okay to kill someone, there are times when people must act in self-defence.

(ii) John Ward should not have been shot dead. _____ , neither should he have been trespassing on the farmer's land.

(iii) There were mitigating circumstances in the farmer's case. _____ the jury was right to convict him the first time.

(iv) _____ the farmer spent six years in jail, many would say he was lucky to escape without a more severe punishment.

(v) It's true; the farmer shot dead John Ward. _____ , he should never have been convicted of murder.

(vi) _____ the fact that the farmer shot John Ward dead, he is a free man today.

(H) Write the correct **definition** beside the **punishment**.

community service _____
prison sentence   *sending the criminal to jail*
life sentence _____
fine _____
suspended sentence _____
asset forfeiture _____
probation _____
the death penalty _____

(i) doing jobs like road seeping and cleaning up rubbish
(ii) sentenced to be killed
(iii) allowing a criminal to remain free under supervision
(iv) sending the criminal to jail
(v) making the criminal pay an amount of money
(vi) a jail sentence that will only apply if the criminal offends again
(vii) taking away the criminal's property and belongings
(viii) sending the criminal to jail for life

(I) Look at the example answer for the question:
'What do you think would be an appropriate sentence for a 13-year-old boy caught stealing a T.V. from a house?'

1 ## Make a statement

If it was up to me, the offender would get community service.

2 ## Explain the statement

I would rather see a young person doing something useful with their time like sweeping roads or cleaning graffiti off public property than watch them learn about crime from fellow prisoners in jail.

3 ## Give an example / support the statement

It is a well-known fact that people who are sent to jail are more likely to become re-offenders or indeed 'career criminals'. Besides, kids are easy to influence - just think what damage it would do to this young offender to be around seasoned criminals all the time; he would surely end up wanting to be like them. That's why, if you think about it, it is much better for the kid to do community service. This way, he can learn the value of hard work and put his time to good use. Moreover, it'll keep him out of trouble!

Now try to answer the following questions with your partner in a similar way: (a) make your statement, (b) explain it, and (c) give reasons or provide examples to support it.

(i)   What do you think would be an appropriate sentence for a serial killer?
(ii) What about a wealthy businessman who tricked elderly people into giving him lots of money, which he used to buy a garage full of fast cars?
(iii) What about a man who beat up another man badly when he found out this other man was having an affair with his wife?
(vi) What about a mother who shot dead an intruder she found in the bedroom of her new-born baby?
(vii) What about a man who drove his car while drunk and ran over a five-year-old girl?
(viii) What about a woman who hid behind a corner and jumped out and shouted 'boo' at her boyfriend, only for her boyfriend to have a heart attack and collapse dead?
(ix) What about someone caught on camera driving over the speed limit?
(x)   What about a man on a boat who got into an argument with another passenger, started to wrestle with the other passenger and accidentally pushed him over the side, where he drowned?

(J) How can we help reduce crime?
Discuss these ideas with your partner and rank them from 1-5, 1 being the best idea.

(i) Train people in jail with new skills.   ____
(ii) Put more police on the streets.   ____
(iii) Send more criminals to prison.   ____
(vi) Have more serious punishments for crime.   ____
(v) Improve the education system so that all young people have equal opportunities. ____

Do you have any ideas of your own? Write down as many as you can think of in the box, then discuss them with your partner and decide on four or five really good ideas to share with the class. *Share your ideas with the rest of the class.*

_____
_____
_____
_____

Stock phrases: Contrasting your opinion with what most people think.

If you think that your opinion is unusual or that most people would disagree with you, here are some ways to help you express this notion:

(i) For many/most/some people... but I believe...
(ii) To many/most/some people... but to me...
(iii) Many/most/some believe... but I...
(iv) Many/most/some would say... but I...

(v) A lot of people think... but I beg to differ.
(vi) For some people... but for me...
(vii) I differ from a lot of people in that I believe...
(viii) You might expect me to say/think... but actually...

(K) Look at the following statement.

Murderers should be sent to prison for life.

Most of us would probably agree with that statement. However, for the sake of this exercise, we are going to disagree.

Question: *Do you think that murderers should be sent to prison for life?*

1 Most people believe that murderers should be sent to prison for life but I would have to disagree.

2 I mean, prison these days is quite a nice, comfortable, safe place. It's not really much of a punishment now, is it? I think a life of hard labour is a far more suitable sentence.

3 Why hard labour? Well, think about it; the criminal would be made to work very hard every day to pay for what he had done, so it is a good form of punishment. But not only that, he would also be making an important contribution to society - his life would have some value. On the other hand, if he just sat in his prison cell for the next 25 years, what good would that be to anyone?

Now it's your turn. For each of the following questions, you MUST argue an unusual opinion. For the moment, write your answers using the three-step principle (make statement - explain statement - support statement), and use the linking expressions you have learnt to bring each answer together.

(i) Do you think it is fair to treat young child criminals under the age of ten the same as adults? [Yes, it is...]

_____
_____
_____
_____
_____
_____

(ii) Do you think people caught shoplifting should be sentenced to life in prison? [Yes, they should...]

_____
_____
_____
_____
_____
_____

(iii) Do you think criminals should be allowed to keep the things they steal? [Of course...]

_____
_____
_____
_____
_____
_____

(iv) Should people who are very bad at parking their cars be arrested? [Definitely...]

_____
_____
_____
_____
_____
_____

(v) Do you think students who don't do their homework should be sentenced to community service?
   [Of course they should/ I do...]

_____
_____
_____
_____
_____
_____

(vi) Do you think it is a good idea to close all prisons and release all criminals back out onto the street?
   [Absolutely...]

_____
_____
_____
_____
_____
_____

Now, with a partner, ask each other the questions again. Don't read or look at your answers. Simply speak.

Stock phrases: **When you are asked a question, you may not want to totally agree or disagree, or you may not have a 'Yes or No' answer. Maybe you see both sides of the argument, or maybe it depends on the situation.**

When that is the case, here are some stock phrases you can use to help you:

(i) In some circumstance.... In others....
(ii) To some extent... but...
(iii) Some believe... while others...
(iv) Some would say... while others...
(v) In some cases... In other cases...
(vi) Sometimes... Having said that...
(vii) For some people... For others...
(viii) That can varying according to the situation.

The phrase That depends. is perhaps the simplest one of all which you can use in this situation. Or, indeed, the related phrase, It depends on the situation.

IELTS Speaking

(L) Look at the following statement.

Children (under the age of 18) should never be sent to prison.

Most of us would probably agree with that statement. But in the case of a serious crime like murder, does it matter how old you are? It probably depends on the circumstances...

Question: **_Do you think it is wrong to send a person under the age of 18 to prison?_**

1 _I think it very much depends on the situation._

2 _In some circumstances, where the crime is very serious, you might have to send a child to jail. In others, where the child is very young, or, of course, if the crime is not very bad , it would be wrong to._

3 _Take, for example, a 17-year-old who gets his dad's gun and walks into school one day and starts shooting everybody. Is a 17-year-old mature enough to know what he is doing? Absolutely. Should he be made to pay for his crimes? One hundred percent yes. On the other hand, what about a three-year-old who finds his dad's gun and thinks it's a toy. He points and shoots it at his mother. She is killed. Of course, it would simply be ridiculous to send this kid to jail._

Now it's your turn. For each of the following questions, you MUST argue both sides. For the moment, write your answers using the three-step principle (make statement - explain statement - support statement), and use the linking expressions (expressions of contrast are particularly useful in this case when you are supporting your statement as you are showing two sides to something) you have learnt to bring each answer together.

(i) 'All murderers should spend life in prison'. Would you agree?

_____

_____

_____

_____

_____

(ii) Do you think it is a good idea to put more police patrols on the streets?

_____

_____

_____

_____

_____

(iii) If you hit me, I have a right to hit you back. Do you agree?

_____

_____

_____

_____

_____

Now, with a partner, ask each other the questions again. Don't read or look at your answers. Simply speak.

Speaking Test 9

Part 1

The examiner will ask you some questions about yourself.

Let's talk about Money.

Where do you get the money you need to buy things?

What do you do when you need more money?

What sorts of things do you buy for yourself?

Do you think you are good with money?

What is the most expensive thing you ever bought?

The examiner will then ask you some questions about one or two other topics. See the example below.

Now let's talk about Your Possessions.

What is your most important possession?

What is your most valuable possession?

What sorts of presents do you like to receive?

What is the best present you ever got?

Have you ever taken anything that was not yours?

Have any of your possessions ever been lost or stolen?

Part 2

The examiner will give you a topic on a card like the one below and ask you to talk about it for one to two minutes. Before you talk you have one minute to think about what you want to say. The examiner will give you some paper and a pencil so you can make notes if you want to.

> Describe a time when you got in trouble for something
> You should say:
> - where you were and what you did wrong
> - why you did it
> - how you were punished
>
> and whether or not you think the punishment was fair.

The examiner may ask you one or two more related questions when you have finished, like those given in the example below.

Do you think you would ever commit a crime?

Have you ever been the victim of a crime (or known someone who has been)?

Have you ever been in a fight? Was it serious? Why were you fighting?

Part 3

The examiner will ask you some more general questions which follow on from the topic in Part 2.

Do you think murderers deserve the death penalty?

How can we help reduce the level of crime?

Is the statement, 'Once a criminal, always a criminal', true?

Is there a link between crime and poverty?

What is wrong with sending a young offender to prison, if anything?

Are there good alternatives to prison?

Do you think the same rules of law apply for rich people as for poor people?

Unit 10 Health

(A) Look at the picture. This person is obese, a way of saying that they are so overweight that it is dangerous to their health. All across the developed world obesity is becoming a serious issue.
Can you think what the reasons for this might be?

Before answering this question, think about the following:
- *In most families, how many parents work?*
- *Do working parents have time to cook food?*
- *What food is easy to prepare?*
- *Do a lot of people work in offices today?*
- *Do people who work in offices have very active days?*
- *What sorts of hobbies do children have today?*
- *Do they play a lot of computer games?*
- *Do they watch a lot of T.V.?*
- *Do they lead very active lives?*
- *Are children influenced by advertising?*
- *What types of food are advertised the most?*
- *What types of food cost the most in shops?*
- *What types of food are the least expensive?*

Hopefully, this list of questions should have helped you find the answer(s) to the original one. Now, let's look at that again: **Why is obesity such a big problem today in the developed world?**
Think of as many reasons as you can and write them down in the box below.

> - Most homes have two working parents and they have no time to cook

(B) Compare your list with your partner's. Write down any points you may have missed. Then ask each other these questions.

- Why is fast food so popular today?
- Do we lead more sedentary lifestyles today than in the past?
- What types of food are the best for our health?
- Are healthy foods affordable?
- What problems do obese people have in their day-to-day lives?
- What more serious problems can obesity lead to over time?

> **A sedentary lifestyle**
>
> If you lead a sedentary lifestyle, this means that you are not very active in your day-to-day life. A person who sits in front of a computer all day at work and watches T.V. all evening leads a sedentary lifestyle.

(C) Which of the following foods do you think has the most calories? Put the foods in order from **1-5** based on how many calories you think they contain, **1** being the most calorific.

(i) a doner kebab	(1) _____
(ii) a Big Mac	(2) _____
(iii) a large cola fizzy drink	(3) _____
(iv) 6 chicken wings	(4) _____
(v) a medium pizza	(5) _____

Now compare your answers with your partners and try to justify them. *Then ask your teacher to confirm the actual correct answers.*

(D) Look at the picture. This model is extremely thin.

Discuss the following questions with your partner:

- *Are young girls put under a lot of pressure to look 'good'?*
  Who/what puts pressure on them?
- *Do you think models are of a 'normal', healthy weight?*
- *Why don't magazines use bigger models?*
- *Are 'slim' people more popular?*
- *Do people who are overweight get picked on?*
- *Is being overweight a sign of laziness?*
- *Which is worse; to be slightly underweight or to be slightly overweight?*
- *What problems can be caused by young girls trying to look like models?*

Anorexia

If you are anorexic, you have a fear of becoming fat and do not eat enough food. As a result, you become very weak and thin, and risk death if the condition gets serious.

(E) Read the text below.

Young Smokers

Every year about 165,000 young people take up smoking in Britain; that works out at around 450 a day. In fact, proportionately, more young people smoke than do those aged 30-plus. Nearly one in every ten 11- to 15-year-olds describe themselves as regular smokers. That figure is one in every five for 15-year-olds taken on their own, and, by the age of 19, one quarter of all teens smoke regularly. Alarmingly, only 40% of underage smokers said they found it difficult to purchase cigarettes. That means that 6 in every 10 found it relatively easy to do so, despite the fact that it is illegal for shopkeepers to sell cigarettes to under-18s. Young girls are more likely to have tried a cigarette or become regular smokers than young boys today. More 20- to 25-year-olds smoke in Britain than any other age group.

(i) What evidence is there according to the text to suggest that smoking among young people continues to be a serious problem? Write the evidence down in short points (in note form) below.

1: _____
2: _____
3: _____
4: _____
5: _____
6: _____
7: _____
8: _____

(ii) Now, try to answer the following question:

Smoking amongst young people is not the problem it once was. Do you agree?

Ask your partner the question and then switch roles.
Remember: (1) make a statement, (2) explain the statement, and (3) provide evidence to support your opinion.

IELTS Speaking

(F) Look at the following list. It shows possible reasons why young people might start smoking.

Discuss the list with your partner and decide what the main reasons are. Try to come up with one or two reasons of your own as well.

Peer Pressure

Peer pressure is pressure put on you by people your own age to do something, or a feeling that you should do something because a lot of people your age are doing it.

(i) Parents or siblings are also smokers.
(ii) They think smoking makes them look cool and mature.
(iii) Their friends are doing it.
(iv) Other people their age put pressure on them to smoke.

(v) They smoke to deal with the stress of school.
(vi) _____
(vii) _____

(G) Read the text below.

The root of the problem

Children are three times more likely to smoke if their parents or siblings are smokers. And it seems that it is far too easy for them to find cigarettes, with very few shopkeepers obeying the law and refusing to serve underage children. Another factor in the rise in the number of young smokers is the affordability of cigarettes for young people. These days, young people have a lot of spare cash and can easily afford to pay for the cost of a packet. In a survey of 12- to 15-year-olds carried out recently, it was also found that very few of them were aware of the serious health problems associated with smoking. But for many young people, the decision to smoke is mostly based on what their friends are doing - if their friends smoke, so will they.

(i) List the causes of the problem as identified in the above text in note form. Then write a proposed solution down next to each problem, as in the example.

1:	parents or siblings smoke	⟶	need to get parents and siblings to quit
2:	_____	⟶	_____
3:	_____	⟶	_____
4:	_____	⟶	_____
5:	_____	⟶	_____

(ii) Now try to answer the following question:

How can we get young people to stop smoking?

Ask your partner the question and then switch roles.
Remember: (1) make a statement, (2) explain the statement, and (3) provide evidence to support your opinion.

(H) What are the long-term health problems associated with smoking? Read the text and then list them on the right.

Smoking and Your Health

There are about 4,000 dangerous chemicals in every cigarette. Of these, at least 80 are known to be cancer causing. The most common form of cancer suffered by smokers is of the lungs. However, other types, such as oral and stomach cancer, have also been known to occur. If you smoke, you are also five times more likely to have a heart attack from middle age on, and you are also more prone to suffering a stroke. Smoking during pregnancy can lead to miscarriage and is also related to cot death, the mysterious condition where a seemingly healthy baby dies in its sleep. Regular smokers also risk damaging their reproductive capacity and may become sterile. The ash from cigarettes can sometimes lodge in the eye as well, which can lead to retinal detachment and blindness.

List of Health Problems

(ii) Now try to answer the following question:

What long-term damage to a person's health can smoking cause?

Ask your partner the question and then switch roles.
Remember: (1) make a statement, (2) explain the statement, and (3) provide evidence to support your opinion.

(I) (i) Smoking is a serious addiction. What other types of addictions can you think of? Write them in the space provided below.

_____

_____

_____

(ii) Discuss the following questions with your partner.

    (1) What type of addiction is the most serious?
    (2) What reasons might a person have for drinking a lot?
    (3) Is drug taking a problem in your neighbourhood?
    (4) Is gambling a less serious addiction than drug taking?

Addiction
If you are addicted to something, you do that something regularly and could not easily stop doing it by choice - you keep wanting more and more of it.

(J) Match the words in **Table A** with their meanings in **Table B**.

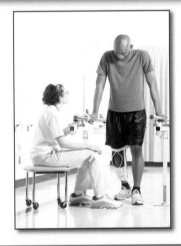

Table A	Table B
sprain	to cause stress and strain to a joint without dislocating it
consultant	the place where a surgeon operates on patients
fracture	someone who receives treatment and leaves hospital the same day
cut	a small break in the bone
scan	a disease that has spread across a large area and affected many people
epidemic	the method a doctor uses to try to help a patient recover to full health
treatment	when you go to the doctor to make sure that you are still healthy
check-up	someone who must remain in hospital for treatment for at least one night
inpatient	a test or examination of part of the body using technology
outpatient	an open, injured area of skin
theatre	a doctor who is an expert in a specific area

(K) Read the following passage and fill in the gaps using the words from the box below.

A Day to Remember

It was the final of the inter-schools soccer tournament, and I had scored two goals playing a blinder in midfield. I was dictating play; passing well; I was on fire. It was turning into one of the best days of my life.

And then it happened. A crunch and snap; someone had come in hard from behind. I felt my leg go from under me and lost **(1)** _____consciousness_____ . When I woke up briefly, I was in an **(2)** _____ or something as far as I could make out. Then I drifted back into sleep again. My mother told me the rest...

I was rushed to **(3)** _____ , with a suspected **(4)** _____ , having been taken off the football field on a **(5)** _____ in a comatose state. Everyone was pretty worried.

The doctors brought me straight into **(6)** _____ and **(7)** _____ ; it was a very bad injury. I had just come to, my mum said, moments before the surgery was about to commence, only for the strong **(8)** _____ to kick in and put me back into a deep, deep sleep. Not only was my lower leg shattered in eight different places, but my knee was **(9)** _____ , too, and had to be put back into position.

For a while, they had thought that they would have to **(10)** _____ , but luckily I had the best doctor in the country looking after me. Thank goodness my mum had taken out **(11)** _____ ; otherwise we would never have been able to afford to go **(12)** _____ for treatment.

I woke up about three hours later, tired and sore, but all in one piece. The doctor kept me in hospital for **(13)** _____ for about a week before I was released. I had **(14)** _____ on my leg and needed to use **(15)** _____ to walk, but at least I still had it! In time, the doctor said, it would be as good as new.

The doctor gave me a **(16)** _____ for some strong **(17)** _____ as he said it would be very sore for a while. He also prescribed some **(18)** _____ to help me get my strength back and some **(19)** _____ to fight infection.

I was very nervous after all the trauma, and perhaps this induced an attack of **(20)** _____ , which I hadn't had since I was eight years old. On seeing my breathing difficulties, the nurse quickly brought me an **(21)** _____ .

What a week this was turning about to be...

broken leg	Accident and Emergency	health insurance
crutches	prescription	consciousness
inhaler	antibiotics	theatre
asthma	painkillers	operated
stretcher	steroids	amputate
dislocated	anaesthetic	observation
ambulance	private	plaster

(L) Talk about the following questions with your partner.

- *Have you ever been badly injured? What happened?*
- *Have you been in hospital before for an operation (or something else)? What happened?*
- *What is the most painful thing that has ever happened to you?*
- *Do you have any ongoing conditions like asthma?*
- *What about allergies - do you have any of those?*

Share your experiences with the rest of the class.
Then discuss these questions as a class, or with your partner.

- *Are there any hospitals in your area?*
- *What is the standard of healthcare like in your country?*
- *Is healthcare expensive in your country?*
- *Do you have private health insurance? Why do people decide to take out private health insurance?*
- *Is the work of a doctor difficult?*
- *Would you like to be one?*
- *Why is the job of a nurse important - what role does he/she play?*

(M) Look at this question:

Should the best medical care be free for all?

(i) Write down as many reasons as you can think of to support each side of the argument, (1) Yes and (2) No, as in the example.

(1) Yes

it's a government service - we pay for it through taxes

_____

_____

_____

_____

_____

_____

(2) No

top-class medical care is extremely expensive - someone

has to pay for it and the government cannot afford to

_____

_____

_____

_____

_____

(ii) Now, try to answer the question. Ask your partner the question and then switch roles.

You should look at both sides of the argument before giving your opinion. Use linking words of contrast to examine both sides of the argument (**On the one hand ... but on the other...** etc.)

Stock Phrases:	When you want to indicate that you have considered both sides of the argument before giving your opinion.

- Weighing everything up, I have come to the conclusion...
- Having looked at it from both sides, I have drawn the conclusion that...
- Taking everything into account, I have concluded that...

- All things considered, I believe...
- Having looked at it from both angles, it now seems to me...
- Taking everything into consideration, I've decided...

(N) Look at the pictures. They show different activities people do to keep fit. Discuss with a partner:

- *What do you do to stay fit and healthy?*
- *Why is exercise important?*
- *What do you think is the best form of exercise?*
- *Is it important to look good?*
- *What are the benefits of leading an active lifestyle?*

(O) Put the activities listed in the box in the right column of the table according to the verb they take. Some can be put in more than one column.

cycling	badminton	hopscotch
karate	rounders	tag
gymnastics	P. E.	rugby
hill walking	fencing	aerobics
athletics	swimming	weights
sky diving	jogging	press-ups
snorkelling	tennis	

Do	Play	Go
Karate		

(P) Look at the pictures. They show different kinds of food. Discuss with a partner:

- *What do you consider a healthy diet?*
- *What foods are particularly good for you?*
- *What foods are particularly bad for you?*
- *Why is maintaining a healthy diet important?*
- *'Everything in moderation.' Do you agree with this idea when it comes to eating?*
- *Do you eat home-cooked meals often?*
- *Which do you think are better for our health - home-cooked meals or bought meals?*
- *Which meal is the most important of the day in your opinion?*

Speaking Test 10

Part 1

The examiner will ask you some questions about yourself.

Let's talk about Your Eating Habits.
How often do you eat fast food?
What's your favourite type of fast food?
Do you snack a lot? What kinds of snacks do you eat?
Do you have breakfast everyday? Why / why not?
What time do you usually eat dinner at?
What do you eat for lunch when you are at school?

The examiner will then ask you some questions about one or two other topics. See the example below.

Now let's talk about Your Health.
What kinds of exercise do you do regularly?
When and how often do you brush your teeth?
Do you play any sports competitively?
When was the last time you went for a check-up at the doctor's? Did you have any problems?
What time do you get to sleep at most nights? How many hours of sleep do you get each night?

Part 2

The examiner will give you a topic on a card like the one below and ask you to talk about it for one to two minutes. Before you talk you have one minute to think about what you want to say. The examiner will give you some paper and a pencil so you can make notes if you want to.

> Describe a time when you had to go to the doctor's/hospital
> You should say:
> ● what was wrong with you
> ● how you felt at the time
> ● what happened at the doctor's/hospital
> and explain what treatment you were given to help you get better.

The examiner may ask you one or two more related questions when you have finished, like those given in the example below.

Do you tend to get sick often?
Have you ever been very seriously ill?
Do you like going to the dentist's?
How regularly do you go for a check-up at the doctor's and dentist's?

Part 3

The examiner will ask you some more general questions which follow on from the topic in Part 2.

Why is obesity such a big problem today?
What needs to be done to stop obesity levels growing?
This country's health system is very good - do you agree?
What could be done to improve the nation's health system?
Does everyone have a right to free healthcare?
Do you think rich people get a better quality of healthcare than poor?
How can eating healthily and exercising regularly benefit your life?